Microsoft®
PowerPoint 2000
Illustrated Basic Edition

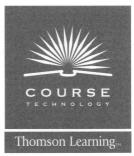

COURSE
TECHNOLOGY

Thomson Learning™

ONE MAIN STREET, CAMBRIDGE, MA 02142

APPROVED COURSEWARE

Australia • Canada • Denmark • Japan • Mexico • New Zealand • Philippines
Puerto Rico • Singapore • South Africa • Spain • United Kingdom • United States

Microsoft PowerPoint 2000 — Illustrated Basic Edition is published by Course Technology

Senior Product Manager:	**Kathryn H. Schooling**
Product Managers:	**Jennifer A. Duffy, Rebecca VanEsselstine**
Associate Product Manager:	**Emily Heberlein**
Author:	**David W. Beskeen**
Contributing Author:	**Barbara Clemens**
Editorial Assistant:	**Stacie Parillo**
Marketing Manager:	**Kristine Murray**
Production Editor:	**Christine Spillett**
Development Editor:	**Katherine T. Pinard**
Composition House:	**GEX, Inc.**
QA Manuscript Reviewers:	**John Freitas, Jeff Schwartz, Alex White**
Text Designer:	**Joseph Lee, Joseph Lee Designs**
Cover Designer:	**Doug Goodman, Doug Goodman Designs**

For more information contact:

Course Technology
One Main Street
Cambridge, MA 02142
Or find us on the World Wide Web at: www.course.com

Trademarks

Disclaimer

ISBN 0-7600-6395-8

Printed in the United States of America

1 2 3 4 5 6 7 8 9 B 04 03 02 01 00

The Illustrated Series Offers the Entire Package for your Microsoft Office 2000 Needs

Office 2000 MOUS Certification Coverage

The Illustrated Series offers a growing number of Microsoft-approved titles that cover the objectives required to pass the Office 2000 MOUS exams. After studying with any of the approved Illustrated titles (see list on inside cover), you will have mastered the Core and Expert skills necessary to pass any Office 2000 MOUS exam with flying colors. In addition, **PowerPoint 2000 MOUS Certification Objectives** at the end of the book map to where specific MOUS skills can be found in each lesson and where students can find additional practice.

Helpful New Features

The Illustrated Series responded to Customer Feedback by adding a **Project Files list** at the back of the book for easy reference, Changing the red font in the Steps to green for easier reading, and Adding New Conceptual lessons to units to give students the extra information they need when learning Office 2000.

New Exciting Case and Innovative On-Line Companion

There is an exciting new case study used throughout our textbooks, a fictitious company called MediaLoft, designed to be "real-world" in nature by introducing the kinds of activities that students will encounter when working with Microsoft Office 2000. The **MediaLoft Web site**, available at www.course.com/illustrated/medialoft, is an innovative Student Online Companion which enhances and augments the printed page by bringing students onto the Web for a dynamic and continually updated learning experience. The MediaLoft site mirrors the case study used throughout the book, creating a real-world intranet site for this chain of bookstore cafés. This Companion is used to complete the WebWorks exercise in each unit of this book, and to allow students to become familiar with the business application of an intranet site.

Enhance Any Illustrated Text with these Exciting Products!

Course CBT

Enhance your students' Office 2000 classroom learning experience with self-paced computer-based training on CD-ROM. Course CBT engages students with interactive multimedia and hands-on simulations that reinforce and complement the concepts and skills covered in the textbook. All the content is aligned with the MOUS (Microsoft Office User Specialist) program, making it a great preparation tool for the certification exams. Course CBT also includes extensive pre- and post-assessments that test students' mastery of skills.

Course Assessment

How well do your students *really* know Microsoft Office? Course Assessment is a performance-based testing program that measures students' proficiency in Microsoft Office 2000. Previously known as SAM, Course Assessment is available for Office 2000 in either a live or simulated environment. You can use Course Assessment to place students into or out of courses, monitor their performance throughout a course, and help prepare them for the MOUS certification exams.

Create Your Ideal Course Package with CourseKits™

If one book doesn't offer all the coverage you need, create a course package that does. With Course Technology's CourseKits—our mix-and-match approach to selecting texts—you have the freedom to combine products from more than one series. When you choose any two or more Course Technology products for one course, we'll discount the price and package them together so your students can pick up one convenient bundle at the bookstore.

For more information about any of these offerings or other Course Technology products, contact your sales representative or visit our web site at:

www.course.com

Preface

Welcome to *Microsoft PowerPoint 2000 – Illustrated Basic Edition!* This book in our highly visual design offers users a hands-on introduction to Microsoft PowerPoint 2000 and also serves as an excellent reference for future use. This book is part of an integrated learning system consisting of two manuals providing progressive training in Microsoft PowerPoint 2000. If you would like additional coverage of PowerPoint 2000, we also offer Illustrated Course Guide *Microsoft PowerPoint 2000-Illustrated Advanced Edition.* These two manuals, when used in conjunction with each other, serve as courseware for the Microsoft Office User Specialist (MOUS) program. After completing the units in these two books, you will be prepared to take the core and expert level MOUS exams for Microsoft PowerPoint 2000. By passing the certification exams, you demonstrate to employers your proficiency in PowerPoint 2000. See more information on MOUS exams and where to find them on the inside cover.

▶ Organization and Coverage

This text contains five units that teach introductory PowerPoint skills. In these units students learn how to create, modify, customize and enhance presentations.

▶ About this Approach

The Illustrated approach is designed to make your workers more productive. It also works to help them retain useful information. The skills your employees learn from these manuals can be immediately applied to their daily tasks. The manuals are an ideal reference tool for after the training is completed, and when used as such, can lower the demands on your internal technical support staff.

Each skill is presented on two facing pages, with the step-by-step instructions on the left page, and large screen illustrations on the right. Students can focus on a single skill without having to turn the page. This unique design makes information extremely accessible and easy to absorb, and provides a great reference after the course. This hands-on approach also makes it ideal for both self-paced or instructor-led classes.

Each lesson, or "information display," contains the following elements:

Each 2-page spread focuses on a single skill.

Clear step-by-step directions explain how to complete the specific task, with what students are to type in red. When students follow the numbered steps, they quickly learn how each procedure is performed and what the results will be.

Concise text that introduces the basic principles discussed in the lesson. Procedures are easier to learn when concepts fit into a framework.

Using the AutoContent Wizard

PowerPoint 2000

When PowerPoint first starts, the startup dialog box opens. The startup dialog box gives you four options for starting your presentation. See Table A-2 for an explanation of all the options in the PowerPoint startup dialog box. The first option, the AutoContent Wizard, is the quickest way to create a presentation. A *wizard* is a series of steps that guides you through a task (in this case, creating a presentation). Using the AutoContent Wizard, you choose a presentation type from the wizard's list of sample presentations. Then you indicate what type of output you want. Next, you type the information for the title slide and the footer. The AutoContent Wizard then creates a presentation with sample text you can use as a guide to help formulate the major points of your presentation. ✒ Maria decides to start her presentation by opening the AutoContent Wizard.

Steps

1. In the startup dialog box, click the **AutoContent Wizard option button** to select it, then click **OK**
   The AutoContent Wizard dialog box opens, as shown in Figure A-5. The left section outlines the contents of the AutoContent Wizard and places a green box next to the current screen name. The text on the right side explains the purpose of the wizard.

Trouble?
If the Office Assistant is in your way, drag it out of the way.

2. Click **Next**
   The Presentation type screen appears. This screen contains category buttons and types of presentations. Each presentation type contains suggested text for a particular use. By default, the presentation types in the General category are listed.

3. Click the category **Sales/Marketing**, click **Selling a Product or Service** in the list on the right, then click **Next**
   The Presentation style screen appears, asking you to choose an output type.

4. If necessary, click the **On-screen presentation option button** to select it, then click **Next**
   The Presentation options screen requests information that will appear on the title slide of the presentation and in the footer at the bottom of each slide.

5. Click in the **Presentation title text box**, then type **Selling MediaLoft Products**

QuickTip
To start the AutoContent Wizard when PowerPoint is already running, click File on the menu bar, click New, click the General tab, then double-click the AutoContent Wizard icon.

6. Press **[Tab]**, then type your name in the Footer text box

7. Make sure the **Date last updated** and **Slide number check boxes** are selected

8. Click **Next**, then click **Finish**
   The AutoContent Wizard opens the presentation based on the Selling a Product or Service presentation type you chose. Sample text for each slide is listed on the left, and the title slide appears on the right side of the screen. Compare your screen to Figure A-6.

About Wizards and the PowerPoint installation

As you use PowerPoint, you may find that not all AutoContent Wizards are available to you. The wizards available depend on your PowerPoint installation. A basic installation gives you a minimal set of wizards, templates, and other features. Some may be installed so that the program requests the CD "on first use" the first time you request that feature. If you find that a feature you want is not installed, insert the Office CD as directed. If you are working on a networked computer or in a lab, see your technical support person for assistance.

Tips as well as trouble-shooting advice right where you need it — next to the step itself.

Clues to Use boxes provide concise information that either expands on one component of the major lesson skill or describes an independent task that is in some way related to the major lesson skill.

Every lesson features large-size, full-color representations of what the students' screen should look like after completing the numbered steps.

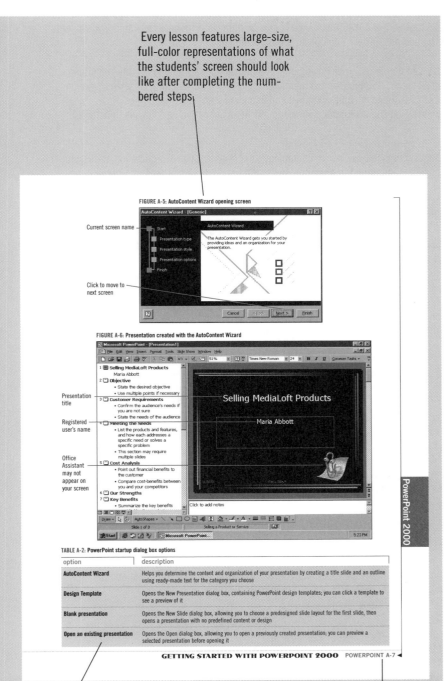

Current screen name

FIGURE A-5: AutoContent Wizard opening screen

Click to move to next screen

FIGURE A-6: Presentation created with the AutoContent Wizard

Presentation title

Selling MediaLoft Products

Registered user's name

Maria Abbott

Office Assistant may not appear on your screen

TABLE A-2: PowerPoint startup dialog box options

option	description
AutoContent Wizard	Helps you determine the content and organization of your presentation by creating a title slide and an outline using ready-made text for the category you choose
Design Template	Opens the New Presentation dialog box, containing PowerPoint design templates; you can click a template to see a preview of it
Blank presentation	Opens the New Slide dialog box, allowing you to choose a predesigned slide layout for the first slide, then opens a presentation with no predefined content or design
Open an existing presentation	Opens the Open dialog box, allowing you to open a previously created presentation; you can preview a selected presentation before opening it

GETTING STARTED WITH POWERPOINT 2000   POWERPOINT A-7 ◄

Quickly accessible summaries of key terms, toolbar buttons, or keyboard alternatives connected with the lesson material. Students can refer easily to this information when working on their own projects at a later time.

The page numbers are designed like a road map. PowerPoint indicates the PowerPoint section, A indicates the first unit, and 7 indicates the page within the unit.

Other Features

The two-page lesson format featured in this book provides the new user with a powerful learning experience. Additionally, this book contains the following features:

► **Real-World Case**
The case study used throughout the text-book, a fictictious company called MediaLoft, is designed to be "real-world" in nature and introduces the kinds of activities that users will encounter when working with Microsoft PowerPoint 2000. With a real-world case, the process of solving problems will be more meaningful. Students can also enhance their skills by completing the Web Works exercises in each unit by going to the innovative Student Online Companion, available at **www.course.com/illustrated/medialoft.** The MediaLoft site mirrors the case study by acting as the company's intranet site, further allowing students to become famil-iar with applicable business scenarios.

► **Practice**
Each unit concludes with a Concepts Review that tests students' understanding of what they learned in the unit. The Concepts Review is followed by a Skills Review, which provides students with additional hands-on practice of the skills they learned in the unit. The Skills Review is followed by Independent Challenges, which pose case problems for students to solve. At least one Independent Challenge in each unit asks students to use the World Wide Web to solve the problem as indicated by a Web Work icon. The Visual Workshops that follow the Independent Challenges help students develop critical thinking skills. Students are shown com-pleted Web pages or screens and are asked to recreate them from scratch.

Instructor's Resource Kit

MediaLoft Web site   Available at www.course.com/illustrated/medialoft, this innovative Student Online Companion enhances and augments the printed page by bringing students onto the Web for a dynamic and continually updated learning experience. The MediaLoft site mirrors the case study used throughout the book, creating a real-world intranet site for this fictional national chain of bookstore cafes. This Companion is used to complete the WebWorks exercise in each unit of this book, and to allow students to become familiar with the business application of an intranet site.

Instructor's Manual   Available as an electronic file, the Instructor's Manual is quality-assurance tested and includes unit overviews, detailed lecture topics for each unit with teaching tips, an Upgrader's Guide, solutions to all lessons and end-of-unit material, and extra Independent Challenges. The Instructor's Manual is available on the Instructor's Resource Kit CD-ROM or you can download it from www.course.com.

Course Test Manager   Designed by Course Technology, this cutting-edge Windows-based testing software helps instructors design, administer, and print tests and pre-tests. A full-featured program, Course Test Manager also has an online testing component that allows students to take tests at the computer and have their exams automatically graded.

Course Faculty Online Companion   You can browse this text's password-protected site to obtain the Instructor's Manual, Solution Files, Project Files, and any updates to the text. Contact your Customer Service Representative for the site address and password.

Project Files   Project Files contain all of the data that students will use to complete the lessons and end-of-unit material. A Readme file includes instructions for using the files. Adopters of this text are granted the right to install the Project Files on any standalone computer or network. The Project Files are available on the Instructor's Resource Kit CD-ROM, the Review Pack, and can also be downloaded from www.course.com.

Solution Files   Solution Files contain every file students are asked to create or modify in the lessons and end-of-unit material. A Help file on the Instructor's Resource Kit includes information for using the Solution Files.

Learning Microsoft Outlook 2000 E-mail   Learning Microsoft Outlook 2000 E-mail is a simulation program designed to mimic the experience of using the mail capabilities of Microsoft Outlook 2000. Using Learning Microsoft Outlook 2000 E-mail, your students will learn to send, receive, forward, and reply to messages, as well as to manage a mailbox. To complete the Microsoft Outlook 2000 unit your students must use a computer that has the Learning Microsoft Outlook 2000 E-mail program installed from either the Review Pack or the Instructor's Resource Kit. Adopters of this text are granted the right to install Learning Microsoft Outlook 2000 E-mail on any standalone computer or network.

CyberClass   CyberClass is a web-based tool designed for on-campus or distance learning. Use it to enhance how you currently run your class by posting assignments and your course syllabus or holding online office hours. Or, use it for your distance learning course, and offer mini-lectures, conduct online discussion groups, or give your mid-term exam. For more information, visit our Web site at: www.course.com/products/cyberclass/index.html.

WebCT   WebCT is a tool used to create Web-based educational environments and also uses WWW browsers as the interface for the course-building environment. The site is hosted on your school campus, allowing complete control over the information. WebCT has its own internal communication system, offering internal e-mail, a Bulletin Board, and a Chat room.

Course Technology offers pre-existing supplemental information to help in your WebCT class creation, such as a suggested Syllabus, Lecture Notes, Figures in the Book/ Course Presenter, Student Downloads, and Test Banks in which you can schedule an exam, create reports, and more.

Contents

Exciting New Features and Products   III
Preface   IV

PowerPoint 2000

Getting Started with PowerPoint 2000   POWERPOINT A-1
Defining Presentation Software...POWERPOINT A-2
Starting PowerPoint 2000 ....POWERPOINT A-4
   Creating a PowerPoint shortcut icon on the desktop.....................POWERPOINT A-4
Using the AutoContent Wizard..POWERPOINT A-6
   About Wizards and the PowerPoint installation............................POWERPOINT A-6
Viewing the PowerPoint Window ....POWERPOINT A-8
   Personalized toolbars and menus in PowerPoint 2000 ....POWERPOINT A-9
Viewing a Presentation ....POWERPOINT A-10
Saving a Presentation ....POWERPOINT A-12
   Saving fonts with your presentation...POWERPOINT A-12
Getting Help ....POWERPOINT A-14
   What do I do if I see a lightbulb on a slide?................................POWERPOINT A-15
Printing and Closing the File, and Exiting PowerPoint ....POWERPOINT A-16
   Viewing your presentation in gray scale or black and white ....POWERPOINT A-17
Concepts Review ....POWERPOINT A-18
Skills Review ....POWERPOINT A-20
Independent Challenges ....POWERPOINT A-21
Visual Workshop ....POWERPOINT A-24

Creating a Presentation   POWERPOINT B-1
Planning an Effective Presentation ....POWERPOINT B-2
Choosing a Look for a Presentation ....POWERPOINT B-4
   Applying a design template to an existing presentation ....POWERPOINT B-5
Entering Slide Text..POWERPOINT B-6
Creating a New Slide ....POWERPOINT B-8
Working in Outline View ....POWERPOINT B-10
Entering Notes...POWERPOINT B-12
   Adding slide footers and headers ....POWERPOINT B-13
Checking Spelling in the Presentation ....POWERPOINT B-14
   Checking spelling as you type...POWERPOINT B-15
Evaluating a Presentation ....POWERPOINT B-16
   Using design templates ....POWERPOINT B-17
Concepts Review ....POWERPOINT B-18
Skills Review ....POWERPOINT B-19
Independent Challenges ....POWERPOINT B-21
Visual Workshop ....POWERPOINT B-24

Modifying a Presentation   POWERPOINT C-1
Opening an Existing Presentation..POWERPOINT C-2
   Searching for a file by properties...POWERPOINT C-3
Drawing and Modifying an Object ....POWERPOINT C-4
   Using the Drawing toolbar ....POWERPOINT C-5
Editing Drawing Objects ....POWERPOINT C-6
   Using the Office Clipboard ....POWERPOINT C-7
Understanding Aligning, Grouping, and Stacking Objects ....POWERPOINT C-8
Aligning and Grouping Objects ....POWERPOINT C-10
   More ways to change objects..POWERPOINT C-11
Adding and Arranging Text ....POWERPOINT C-12

Contents

Inserting slides from other presentations .... POWERPOINT C-12
Importing text from Microsoft Word .... POWERPOINT C-13
Formatting Text .... POWERPOINT C-14
Replacing Text and Attributes .... POWERPOINT C-15
Customizing the Color Scheme and Background .... POWERPOINT C-16
Correcting Text Automatically .... POWERPOINT C-18
Concepts Review .... POWERPOINT C-20
Skills Review .... POWERPOINT C-21
Independent Challenges .... POWERPOINT C-22
Visual Workshop .... POWERPOINT C-24

Enhancing a Presentation   POWERPOINT D-1

Inserting Clip Art .... POWERPOINT D-2
Find more clips online .... POWERPOINT D-3
Inserting, Cropping, and Scaling a Picture .... POWERPOINT D-4
Graphics in PowerPoint .... POWERPOINT D-5
Embedding a Chart .... POWERPOINT D-6
Entering and Editing Data in the Datasheet .... POWERPOINT D-8
Series in Rows vs. Series in Columns .... POWERPOINT D-9
Formatting a Chart .... POWERPOINT D-10
Customizing Charts .... POWERPOINT D-10
Using Slide Show Commands .... POWERPOINT D-12
Creating Tables in PowerPoint .... POWERPOINT D-14
Setting Slide Show Timings and Transitions .... POWERPOINT D-16
Rehearsing slide show timing .... POWERPOINT D-17
Setting Slide Animation Effects .... POWERPOINT D-18
Presentation Checklist .... POWERPOINT D-19
Concepts Review .... POWERPOINT D-20
Skills Review .... POWERPOINT D-21
Independent Challenges .... POWERPOINT D-22
Visual Workshop .... POWERPOINT D-24

Customizing Your Presentation   POWERPOINT E-1

Understanding PowerPoint Masters .... POWERPOINT E-2
Changing the Master Layout .... POWERPOINT E-3
Formatting Master Text .... POWERPOINT E-4
Applying a template from another presentation .... POWERPOINT E-5
Changing Master Text Indents .... POWERPOINT E-6
Exceptions to the Slide Master .... POWERPOINT E-7
Adjusting Text Objects .... POWERPOINT E-8
Changing margins around text in shapes .... POWERPOINT E-9
Using Advanced Drawing Tools .... POWERPOINT E-10
Drawing a freeform shape .... POWERPOINT E-11
Using Advanced Formatting Tools .... POWERPOINT E-12
Applying a color scheme to another presentation .... POWERPOINT E-13
Using the Style Checker .... POWERPOINT E-14
Understanding Style Checker options .... POWERPOINT E-15
Creating and Customizing a Toolbar .... POWERPOINT E-16
Concepts Review .... POWERPOINT E-18
Skills Review .... POWERPOINT E-19
Independent Challenges .... POWERPOINT E-21
Visual Workshop .... POWERPOINT E-24

PowerPoint 2000 MOUS Certification Objectives   1

Glossary   1

Index   4

Getting
Started with PowerPoint 2000

Objectives

- ► **Define presentation software**
- ► **Start PowerPoint 2000**
- MOUS ► **Use the AutoContent Wizard**
- MOUS ► **View the PowerPoint window**
- ► **View a presentation**
- MOUS ► **Save a presentation**
- MOUS ► **Get Help**
- MOUS ► **Print and close the file, and exit PowerPoint**

Microsoft PowerPoint 2000 is a presentation program that transforms your ideas into professional, compelling presentations. With PowerPoint, you can create slides to use as an electronic slide show, as 35-mm slides, and as transparency masters to display on an overhead projector. ✐ Maria Abbott is the general sales manager at MediaLoft, a nationwide chain of bookstore cafés that sells books, CDs, and videos at eight locations. Maria needs to familiarize herself with the basics of PowerPoint and learn how to use PowerPoint to create professional presentations.

Defining Presentation Software

Presentation software is a computer program you use to organize and present information. Whether you are giving a sales pitch or explaining your company's goals and accomplishments, presentation software can help make your presentation effective and professional. You can use PowerPoint to create 35-mm slides, overheads, speaker's notes, audience handouts, outline pages, or on-screen presentations. Table A-1 explains the items you can create using PowerPoint. Maria wants to create a presentation to review sales techniques at a monthly meeting of store managers. She is not familiar with PowerPoint, so she gets right to work exploring its capabilities. Figure A-1 shows an overhead she created using a word processor for a recent presentation. Figure A-2 shows how the same overhead might look in PowerPoint.

Maria can easily complete the following tasks using PowerPoint:

Create slides to display information
With PowerPoint, you can present information on full-color slides with interesting backgrounds, layouts, and clip art. Full-color slides have a more powerful impact than traditional black-and-white overheads.

Enter and edit data easily
Using PowerPoint, you can enter and edit data quickly and efficiently. When you need to change a part of your presentation, you can use the advanced word-processing and outlining capabilities of PowerPoint to edit your content rather than re-create your slides.

Change the appearance of information
By exploring the capabilities of PowerPoint, you will discover how easy it is to change the appearance of your presentation. PowerPoint has many features that can transform the way text, graphics, and slides look.

Organize and arrange information
Once you start using PowerPoint, you won't have to spend a lot of time making sure your information is correct and in the right order. With PowerPoint, you can quickly and easily rearrange and modify any piece of information in your presentation.

Incorporate information from other sources
Often, when you create presentations, you use information from other sources. With PowerPoint, you can import information from spreadsheet, database, and word-processing files prepared in programs such as Microsoft Excel, Microsoft Access, Microsoft Word, and Corel WordPerfect, as well as graphics from a variety of sources.

Show a presentation on any computer running Windows 98 or Windows 95
PowerPoint has a powerful feature called the PowerPoint Viewer that you can use to show your presentation on computers running Windows 98 or Windows 95 that do not have PowerPoint installed. The PowerPoint Viewer displays a presentation as an on-screen slide show.

FIGURE A-1: Traditional overhead

```
Forecast for 2000

- New stores in Austin, Madison,
  and Denver
- 75 new employees
- Sales up 32%
- Expanded CD and video offerings
- Test market online sales
- Another record year!
```

FIGURE A-2: PowerPoint overhead

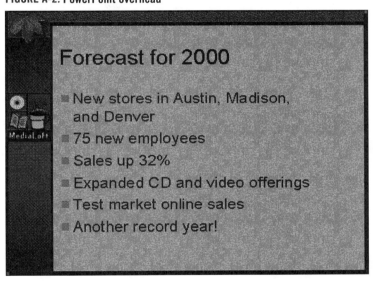

TABLE A-1: Items you can create using PowerPoint

item	use
On-screen presentations	Run a slide show directly from your computer
Web presentations	Broadcast a presentation on the Web or on an intranet that others can view, complete with video and audio
Online meetings	View or work on a presentation with your colleagues in real time
35-mm slides	Use a film-processing bureau to convert PowerPoint slides to 35-mm slides
Black-and-white overheads	Print PowerPoint slides directly to transparencies on your black-and-white printer
Color overheads	Print PowerPoint slides directly to transparencies on your color printer
Speaker notes	Print notes that help you remember points about each slide when you speak to a group
Audience handouts	Print handouts with two, three, or six slides on a page
Outline pages	Print the outline of your presentation to show the main points

Starting PowerPoint 2000

To start PowerPoint, you must first start Windows, and then click the Start button on the taskbar and point to the Programs folder, which usually contains the PowerPoint program icon. If the PowerPoint icon is not in the Programs folder, it might be in a different location on your computer. If you are using a computer on a network, you might need to use a different starting procedure. Maria starts PowerPoint to familiarize herself with the program.

Steps

1. **Make sure your computer is on and the Windows desktop is visible**
   If any program windows are open, close or minimize them.

2. **Click the Start button on the taskbar, then point to Programs**
   The Programs menu opens, showing a list of icons and names for all your programs, as shown in Figure A-3. Your screen might look different, depending on which programs are installed on your computer.

   Trouble?

   If you have trouble finding Microsoft PowerPoint on the Programs menu, check with your instructor or technical support person.

3. **Click Microsoft PowerPoint on the Programs menu**
   PowerPoint starts, and the PowerPoint startup dialog box opens, as shown in Figure A-4. This allows you to choose how you want to create your presentation or to open an existing presentation.

4. **If a dialog balloon connected to the Office Assistant appears, click OK to close it**

Creating a PowerPoint shortcut icon on the desktop

You can make it easier to start PowerPoint by placing a shortcut on the desktop. To create the shortcut, click the Start button, then point to Programs. On the Programs menu, point to Microsoft PowerPoint, then right-click Microsoft PowerPoint. In the pop-up menu that appears, click Create Shortcut. Windows places a shortcut icon named PowerPoint (2) on the Programs menu. Drag this icon to your desktop where it will look like 📖. In the future, you can start PowerPoint by simply double-clicking this icon, instead of using the Start menu. You can edit or change the name of the shortcut by right-clicking the shortcut icon, clicking Rename on the pop-up menu, and then editing as you would any item name in Windows.

FIGURE A-3: Programs menu

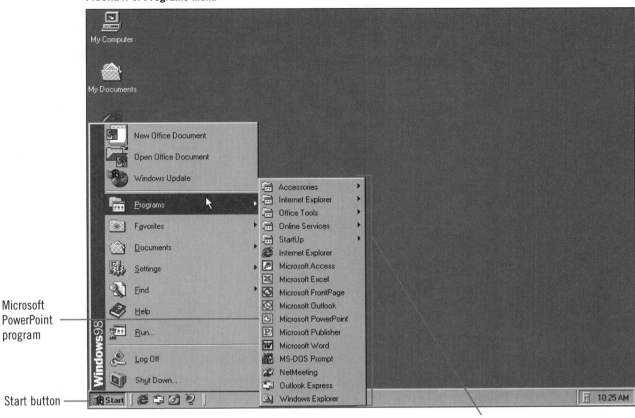

Microsoft
PowerPoint
program

Start button

Your list of programs
will be different

FIGURE A-4: PowerPoint startup dialog box

A different option
may be selected on
your screen

Recently used files
will be listed here

Using the AutoContent Wizard

When PowerPoint first starts, the startup dialog box opens. The startup dialog box gives you four options for starting your presentation. See Table A-2 for an explanation of all the options in the PowerPoint startup dialog box. The first option, the AutoContent Wizard, is the quickest way to create a presentation. A **wizard** is a series of steps that guides you through a task (in this case, creating a presentation). Using the AutoContent Wizard, you choose a presentation type from the wizard's list of sample presentations. Then you indicate what type of output you want. Next, you type the information for the title slide and the footer. The AutoContent Wizard then creates a presentation with sample text you can use as a guide to help formulate the major points of your presentation. ✎ Maria decides to start her presentation by opening the AutoContent Wizard.

Steps

1. In the startup dialog box, click the **AutoContent Wizard option button** to select it, then click **OK**

The AutoContent Wizard dialog box opens, as shown in Figure A-5. The left section outlines the contents of the AutoContent Wizard and places a green box next to the current screen name. The text on the right side explains the purpose of the wizard.

Trouble?

If the Office Assistant is in your way, drag it out of the way.

2. Click **Next**

The Presentation type screen appears. This screen contains category buttons and types of presentations. Each presentation type contains suggested text for a particular use. By default, the presentation types in the General category are listed.

3. Click the category **Sales/Marketing**, click **Selling a Product or Service** in the list on the right, then click **Next**

The Presentation style screen appears, asking you to choose an output type.

4. If necessary, click the **On-screen presentation option button** to select it, then click **Next**

The Presentation options screen requests information that will appear on the title slide of the presentation and in the footer at the bottom of each slide.

5. Click in the **Presentation title text box**, then type **Selling MediaLoft Products**

QuickTip

To start the AutoContent Wizard when PowerPoint is already running, click File on the menu bar, click New, click the General tab, then double-click the AutoContent Wizard icon.

6. Press **[Tab]**, then type your name in the Footer text box

7. Make sure the **Date last updated** and **Slide number check boxes** are selected

8. Click **Next**, then click **Finish**

The AutoContent Wizard opens the presentation based on the Selling a Product or Service presentation type you chose. Sample text for each slide is listed on the left, and the title slide appears on the right side of the screen. Compare your screen to Figure A-6.

About Wizards and the PowerPoint installation

As you use PowerPoint, you may find that not all AutoContent Wizards are available to you. The wizards available depend on your PowerPoint installation. A basic installation gives you a minimal set of wizards, templates, and other features. Some may be installed so that the program requests the CD "on first use" the first time you request that feature. If you find that a feature you want is not installed, insert the Office CD as directed. If you are working on a networked computer or in a lab, see your technical support person for assistance.

FIGURE A-5: AutoContent Wizard opening screen

Current screen name

Click to move to
next screen

FIGURE A-6: Presentation created with the AutoContent Wizard

Presentation
title

Registered
user's name

Office
Assistant
may not
appear on
your screen

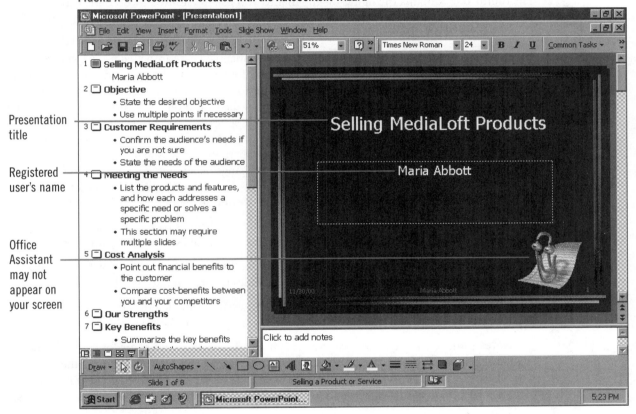

TABLE A-2: PowerPoint startup dialog box options

option	description
AutoContent Wizard	Helps you determine the content and organization of your presentation by creating a title slide and an outline using ready-made text for the category you choose
Design Template	Opens the New Presentation dialog box, containing PowerPoint design templates; you can click a template to see a preview of it
Blank presentation	Opens the New Slide dialog box, allowing you to choose a predesigned slide layout for the first slide, then opens a presentation with no predefined content or design
Open an existing presentation	Opens the Open dialog box, allowing you to open a previously created presentation; you can preview a selected presentation before opening it

Viewing the PowerPoint Window

After you make your selection in the PowerPoint startup dialog box, the Presentation window opens within the PowerPoint window, and the presentation you just created or opened appears. PowerPoint has different **views** that allow you to see your presentation in different forms. By default, the PowerPoint window opens in **Normal view**, which is divided into three **panes** or sections: the Outline pane, the Notes pane, and the Slide pane. Each pane is described below. You move around in each pane by using its scroll bars. Maria examines the elements of the PowerPoint window. Find and compare the elements described below, using Figure A-7 as a guide.

 The **title bar** contains the program name, the title of the presentation, a program Control Menu button, resizing buttons, and the program Close button.

 The **menu bar** contains the names of the menus you use to choose PowerPoint commands, as well as the resizing and Close buttons for the maximized presentation window. When you click a menu name, a list of commands from which you can choose opens.

 The **toolbar** contains buttons for commonly used commands. There are actually two toolbars in this row: **Standard**, which contains buttons for the most frequently used commands, such as copying and pasting; and **Formatting**, which contains buttons for the most frequently used formatting commands, such as changing font type and size, as well as the Common Tasks drop-down menu. The **Common Tasks menu** contains three tasks typically performed in PowerPoint: New Slide, Slide Layout, and Assign Design Template. The Common Tasks menu button may be the only button visible on the Formatting toolbar. By default, the two toolbars appear on one row on your screen when PowerPoint first opens. The contents of the toolbars change depending on which options you have recently selected, but you can reset the toolbars back to their default options if you wish. Be sure to read the Clues to Use in this lesson to learn more about working with PowerPoint's toolbars.

 The **Presentation window** contains the Outline, Slide, and Notes panes. It is the "canvas" where you type text, organize your content, work with lines and shapes, and view your presentation.

 The **Outline pane** displays your presentation text in the form of an outline, without graphics. In this pane, it is easy to move text on or among slides by dragging to reorder the information.

 The **Slide pane** contains the current slide in your presentation, including all text and graphics. You can use this pane's vertical scroll bar to view other slides in the presentation.

 The **Notes pane** lets you type in speaker notes for any slide. Speaker notes are for your reference as you make a presentation, such as reminders of other points you want to make during the presentation. They are not visible to the audience when you make a slide presentation. You can print a copy of your presentation with your notes showing under each slide and refer to this copy as you speak.

 The **Office Assistant** is an animated character that provides help. The character on your screen might be different. You can hide the Office Assistant, but it will reappear if you use the Help system. If another user turned off the Office Assistant, it may not appear on your screen. When the Office Assistant has a style tip, a light bulb appears in the presentation window.

 The **Drawing toolbar**, located below the Presentation window, contains buttons and menus that let you create lines, shapes, and special effects.

 The **view buttons**, at the bottom of the Outline pane, allow you to quickly switch between PowerPoint views.

 The **status bar**, located at the bottom of the PowerPoint window, shows messages about what you are doing and seeing in PowerPoint, including which slide you are viewing.

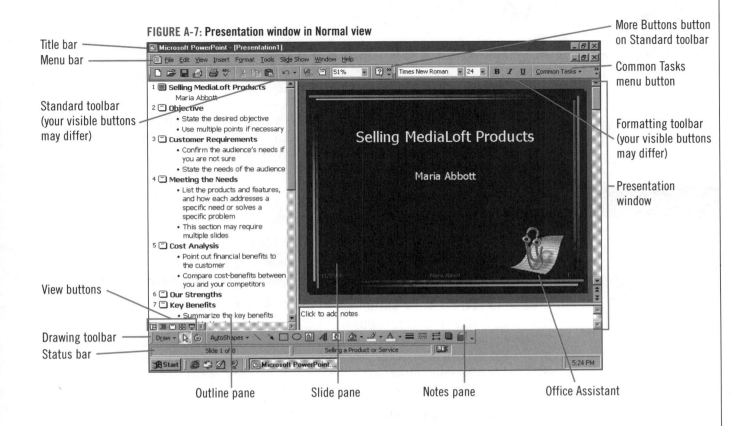

FIGURE A-7: Presentation window in Normal view

Title bar

Menu bar

Standard toolbar (your visible buttons may differ)

View buttons

Drawing toolbar

Status bar

More Buttons button on Standard toolbar

Common Tasks menu button

Formatting toolbar (your visible buttons may differ)

Presentation window

Outline pane

Slide pane

Notes pane

Office Assistant

Personalized toolbars and menus in PowerPoint 2000

PowerPoint toolbars and menus modify themselves to your working style. The Standard and Formatting toolbars you see when you first start PowerPoint include the most frequently used buttons. To locate a button not visible on a toolbar, click the **More Buttons button** at the right end of each toolbar to see the list of additional toolbar buttons. (Because the Standard and Formatting toolbars are on the same line, there are two More Buttons buttons in the row below the menu bar, one for the Standard toolbar and one for the Formatting toolbar.) Throughout the lessons in this book, you will need to remember to click the More Buttons button if a button you are instructed to click is not visible on your screen. As you work, PowerPoint adds the buttons you use to the visible toolbars, and moves the buttons you haven't used in a while to the More Buttons list. Similarly,

PowerPoint menus adjust to your work habits. Short menus appear when you first click a menu command. To view additional menu commands, point to the double-arrow at the bottom of the menu, leave the pointer on the menu name after you've clicked the menu, or double-click the menu name. You can return toolbars and menus to their default settings. Click Tools on the menu bar, click Customize, then click the Options tab in the Customize dialog box. On the Options tab, click Reset my usage data. An alert box or the Office Assistant appears asking if you are sure you want to do this. Click Yes to close the alert box or the dialog balloon, then click Close in the Customize dialog box. Resetting your usage data erases changes made automatically to your menus and toolbars. It does not affect the options you customize.

PowerPoint 2000

Viewing a Presentation

This lesson introduces you to the six PowerPoint views: Normal view, Slide view, Outline view, Slide Sorter view, Notes Page view, and Slide Show view. Each PowerPoint view shows your presentation in a different way and allows you to manipulate your presentation differently. To move easily among the PowerPoint views, use the view buttons located to the left of the horizontal scroll bar, as shown in Figure A-8. Table A-3 provides a brief description of the PowerPoint view buttons and views. ➤ Maria examines each PowerPoint view, starting with Normal view.

Steps

1. **In the Outline pane, click the small slide icon ▭ next to slide 3 to view the Customer Requirements slide in the Slide pane**
   Notice that in Normal view you can easily view the Outline, Slide, and Notes panes.

2. **Click the Previous Slide button ⌃ at the bottom of the vertical scroll bar twice so that slide 1 (the title slide) appears**
   The scroll box in the vertical scroll bar moves back up the scroll bar. The gray slide icon in the Outline pane indicates which slide is displayed in the Slide pane. Both the status bar and the Outline pane indicate the number of the slide you are viewing. As you scroll through the presentation, notice the sample text on each slide created by the AutoContent Wizard.

3. **Click the Outline View button ▤ to the left of the horizontal scroll bar**
   PowerPoint switches to Outline view, which is simply the Outline pane enlarged. See Figure A-8. The Slide pane contains a miniature view of the selected slide.

4. **Click the Slide View button ▫**
   The Slide pane enlarges, the Notes pane disappears, and the Outline pane is reduced to a list of slide numbers and icons that you can click to view other slides. Compare your screen to Figure A-9.

   QuickTip

   Double-click any slide in Slide Sorter view to return to that slide in the previous view.

5. **Click the Slide Sorter View button ▦**
   A miniature image of each slide in the presentation appears in this view. You can examine the flow of your slides and easily move them to change their order.

6. **Click the Slide Show button ▭**
   The first slide fills the entire screen. In this view, you can practice running through your slides as they would appear in an electronic slide show.

7. **Click the left mouse button, press [Enter], or press [Spacebar] to advance through the slides one at a time until you see a black slide, then click once more to return to Slide Sorter view**
   After you view the last slide in Slide Show view, a black slide indicating that the slide show is finished appears. When you click the black slide (or press [Spacebar] or [Enter]), you automatically return to Slide Sorter view, the view you were in before you ran the slide show.

   QuickTip

   To switch to Notes Page view, you must choose Notes Page from the View menu. To switch to Slide and Outline views, you must use the view buttons.

8. **Click View on the menu bar, then click Notes Page**
   Notes Page view appears, showing a reduced image of the title slide above a large box. You can enter text in this box and then print the notes page for your own use to help you remember important points about your presentation.

FIGURE A-8: Outline View

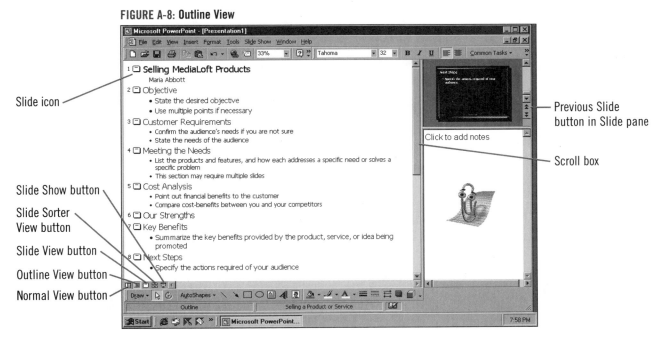

Slide icon

Slide Show button

Slide Sorter
View button

Slide View button

Outline View button

Normal View button

Previous Slide
button in Slide pane

Scroll box

FIGURE A-9: Slide view

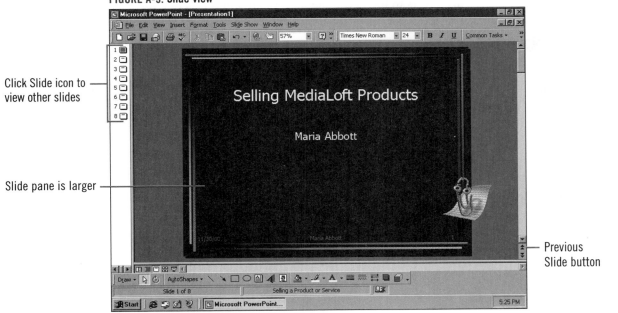

Click Slide icon to
view other slides

Slide pane is larger

Previous
Slide button

PowerPoint 2000

TABLE A-3: View buttons

button	button name	description
	Normal View	Displays the Outline, Slide, and Notes panes at the same time; use this view to work on your presentation's content, layout, and notes concurrently
	Outline View	Widens the outline pane to view the title and main topics in the form of an outline; use this view to enter and edit the text of your presentation
	Slide View	Widens the slide pane so it occupies most of the presentation window; displays one slide at a time; use this view to modify slide content and enhance a slide's appearance
	Slide Sorter View	Displays a miniature picture of all slides in the order in which they appear in your presentation; use this view to rearrange and add special effects to your slides
	Slide Show	Displays your presentation as an electronic slide show

Saving a Presentation

To store your presentation permanently, you must save it as a file on a disk. As a general rule, you should save your work about every 10 or 15 minutes and before printing. You use the Save As command on the File menu to save your presentation for the first time or to save an existing presentation under a different name. Use the Save command to save your changes to a file without changing its name. In this lesson, you save your presentation to your Project Disk. Maria saves her presentation as "Sales Presentation."

Steps

1. **Click File on the menu bar, then click Save As**
   The Save As dialog box opens. See Figure A-10.

2. **Make sure your Project Disk is in the appropriate drive, click the Save in list arrow, then click the drive that contains your Project Disk**
   A default filename placeholder, which PowerPoint takes from the presentation title you entered, appears in the File name text box. If your disk contains any PowerPoint files, their filenames appear in the white area in the center of the dialog box.

Trouble?
Don't worry if you see the extension .ppt after the filename in the title bar or in the list of filenames, even though you didn't type it. Windows can be set up to show or not show the file extensions.

3. **In the File name text box, drag to select the default presentation name if necessary, type Sales Presentation, then click Save**
   Windows 98 allows you to have filenames up to 255 characters long and permits you to use lower- or uppercase letters, symbols, numbers, and spaces. The Save As dialog box closes, and the new filename appears in the title bar at the top of the Presentation window. You decide you want to save the presentation in Outline view instead of in Notes Page view.

4. **Click the Outline View button** 🔳
   The presentation view changes from Notes Page view to Outline view.

QuickTip
To save a file quickly, you can press the shortcut key combination [Ctrl][S].

5. **Click the Save button** 🔲 **on the Standard toolbar**
   The Save command saves any changes you made to the file to the same location you specified when you used the Save As command. Save your file frequently while working with it to protect the presentation.

CLUES TO USE

Saving fonts with your presentation

When you create a presentation, it uses the fonts that are installed on your computer. If you need to open the presentation on another computer, the fonts might look different if that computer has a different set of fonts. To preserve the look of your presentation on any computer, you can save, or **embed**, the fonts in your presentation. Click File on the menu bar, then click Save As. The Save As dialog box opens. Click Tools, then click Embed TrueType fonts from the drop-down list. Finally, click Save. Now the presentation will look the same on any computer that opens it. This option, however, significantly increases the size of your presentation on disk, so only use this option when necessary. You can freely embed any TrueType font that comes with Windows. You can embed other TrueType fonts only if they have no license restrictions.

FIGURE A-10: **Save As dialog box**

Current drive (yours may differ)

Powerpoint files on your current drive are listed here

Step 3

Step 2

Click to save file

PowerPoint 2000

Getting Help

PowerPoint has an extensive Help system that gives you immediate access to definitions, reference information, and feature explanations. Help information appears in a separate window that you can move and resize. Maria likes the way the AutoContent Wizard helped her create a presentation quickly, and she decides to find out more about it.

Trouble?

If the Microsoft PowerPoint Help dialog box opens instead of the Office Assistant, someone turned the Office Assistant off. Click the Close button in the Help window, click Help on the menu bar, click Show the Office Assistant, then repeat step 1. If there is no space in the dialog balloon to type the question, click OK, then repeat Step 1.

1. Click **Help** on the menu bar, then click **Microsoft PowerPoint Help**

If the Office Assistant wasn't already open, it opens. A balloon-shaped dialog box opens near the Office Assistant. The dialog balloon may contain a tip related to the current slide. The question "What would you like to do?" appears at the top of the dialog balloon. It also contains topics related to what is currently on-screen and the last few commands you executed. Below this list is a space for you to type your question. Finally, at the bottom of the dialog balloon are two buttons. Clicking the Options button opens a dialog box that allows you to change Office Assistant options. Clicking the Search button searches PowerPoint Help topics for topics related to the question you type.

2. Type **AutoContent Wizard**, then click **Search**

The dialog balloon closes and reopens with five topics related to the AutoContent Wizard listed under "What would you like to do?" See Figure A-11. If you click the See more option, two more topics appear. The mouse pointer changes to 🖑 when it is positioned over the topics.

QuickTip

To quickly open the Office Assistant dialog balloon, click the animated character, click the Microsoft PowerPoint Help button 🔃 on the Standard toolbar, or press [F1].

3. Click **Create a new presentation**

The Microsoft PowerPoint Help window opens, containing information about creating a new presentation. See Figure A-12. Read the information in the window.

4. Click **Create a presentation based on suggested content and design** in the Microsoft PowerPoint Help window

You may need to scroll down to see this. Another Help window opens listing the steps to follow for using the AutoContent Wizard. Read through the steps.

5. Click the **Show button** 🔲 at the top of the window

The Help window expands to include three tabs: Contents, Answer Wizard, and Index. The Contents tab contains Help topics organized in outline form. To open a Help window about a topic, double-click it. On the Answer Wizard tab, you can search for a key word in all the Help topics. The Index tab contains an alphabetical list of Help topics. Type the word you want help on in text box 1, and the list in box 2 scrolls to that word. Click Search to view related subjects in text box 3, then click the topic you want to read about.

6. Click the **Close button** on the Microsoft PowerPoint Help Window to close it

The Help Topics dialog box closes, and you return to your presentation. The rest of the figures in this text will not show the Office Assistant.

QuickTip

To turn off the Office Assistant completely, right-click the Assistant, click Options, deselect the Use the Office Assistant checkbox, then click OK.

7. Click **Help** on the menu bar, then click **Hide the Office Assistant**

If you have hidden the Office Assistant several times, it may open a dialog balloon asking if you want to turn it off permanently.

8. If a dialog balloon opens asking if you want to turn off the Office Assistant permanently, click the option you prefer in the Office Assistant dialog balloon, then click **OK**

Selecting Hide the Office Assistant only hides it temporarily; it will reappear later to give you tips.

FIGURE A-11: Office Assistant dialog balloon

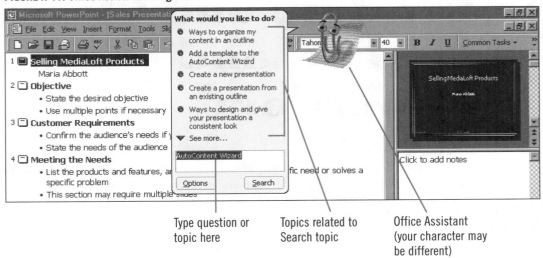

Type question or topic here

Topics related to Search topic

Office Assistant (your character may be different)

FIGURE A-12: Help window

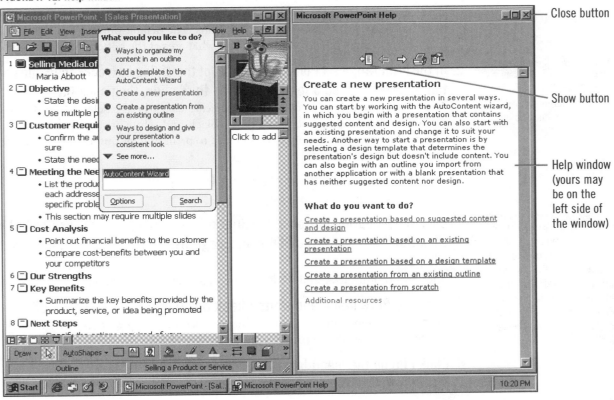

Close button

Show button

Help window (yours may be on the left side of the window)

CLUES TO USE

What do I do if I see a lightbulb on a slide?

If you have the Office Assistant on, you may see a yellow lightbulb in your presentation window. The lightbulb is part of the PowerPoint Help system and it can mean several things. First, the Office Assistant might have a suggestion for appropriate clip art for that slide. Second, the Office Assistant might have a helpful tip based on the task you are performing. This is known as a context-sensitive tip. Third, the Office Assistant might have detected a style, such as a word in the slide title that should be capitalized, which is inconsistent with preset style guidelines. When you see a lightbulb, you can click it, read the dialog balloon, then click the option you prefer, or you can ignore it. If the Office Assistant is hidden or turned off, the lightbulbs do not appear.

Printing and Closing the File, and Exiting PowerPoint

You print your presentation when you have completed it or when you want to review your work. Reviewing hard copies of your presentation at different stages of production gives you an overall perspective of its content and look. When you are finished working on your presentation, close the file containing your presentation and exit PowerPoint. ✐ Maria needs to go to a meeting, so after saving her presentation, she prints the slides and notes pages of the presentation so she can review them later; then she closes the file and exits PowerPoint.

Steps

1. **Click File on the menu bar, then click Print**
   The Print dialog box opens, similar to Figure A-13. In this dialog box, you can specify which slide format you want to print (slides, audience handouts, notes pages, etc.) as well as the number of pages to print and other print options. The default option, Slides, and the Grayscale check box are already selected in the Print what area at the bottom of the dialog box.

> **QuickTip**
> If the Office Assistant appears offering you help with printing, click No in the dialog balloon.

2. **In the Print range section in the middle of the dialog box, click the Slides option button to select it, type 3 to print only the third slide, then click OK**
   The third slide prints. Because the Grayscale check box is selected by default, the black background does not print. If you have a black-and-white printer, the slide prints in shades of gray. To save paper, it's often a good idea to print in handout format, which lets you print up to nine slides per page.

3. **Click File on the menu bar, then click Print**
   The Print dialog box opens again.

> **QuickTip**
> The options you choose in the Print dialog box remain there until you close the presentation. To quickly print the presentation with the current Print options, click the Print button 🖨 on the Standard toolbar.

4. **Click the All option button in the Print range section, click the Print what list arrow, click Handouts, click the Slides per page list arrow in the Handouts section, then click 6**
   The PowerPoint black-and-white option can help you save toner.

5. **Click the Pure black and white check box to select it, then click OK**
   The presentation prints as audience handouts on two pages. If you have a black-and-white printer, the presentation prints without any gray tones.

6. **Click File on the menu bar, then click Print**
   The Print dialog box opens again.

> **QuickTip**
> To print slides in a size appropriate for overhead transparencies, click File, click Page Setup, and click the Slides sized for list arrow. Select Overhead. Then print or copy your slides onto transparency film.

7. **Click the Print what list arrow, click Outline View, then click OK**
   The presentation outline prints. Notice that you can print any view from the Print dialog box, regardless of the current view.

8. **Click File on the menu bar, then click Close**
   If you have made changes to your presentation, a Microsoft PowerPoint alert box opens asking you if you want to save changes you have made to the Sales Presentation file, as shown in Figure A-14.

9. **If necessary, click Yes to close the alert box**

10. **Click File on the menu bar, then click Exit**
    The Presentation window and the PowerPoint program close, and you return to the Windows desktop.

FIGURE A-13: Print dialog box

Your printer name
may be different

Step 2

Step 5

FIGURE A-14: Save changes alert box

Viewing your presentation in gray scale or black and white

Viewing your presentation in pure black and white or in grayscale (using shades of gray) is very useful when you will be printing a presentation on a black-and-white printer and you want to make sure your text will be readable. To see how your color presentation looks in grayscale when you are in any view (except Slide Show View), click the Grayscale Preview button on the Standard toolbar. To see how your slide looks in pure black and white, hold down [Shift] and press, which is now called the Pure Black and White button. If you don't like the way an object looks in black and white or grayscale view, you can change its shading. Right-click a slide object, point to Black and White, and choose from the options on the pop-up menu.

Practice

► Concepts Review

Label the elements of the PowerPoint window shown in Figure A-15.

FIGURE A-15

Match each term with the statement that describes it.

11. **AutoContent Wizard**   c   **a.** The area where you work on your presentation

12. **Presentation window**   a   **b.** Shows slide numbers and small slide icons

13. **Slide Sorter view**   e   **c.** Series of dialog boxes that guides you through creating a presentation and produces a presentation with suggestions for content

14. **Normal view**   d

15. **Outline pane**   b   **d.** Displays the Outline, Slide, and Notes panes

                                   e. Shows all your slides in the same window

Select the best answer from the list of choices.

16. **PowerPoint can help you create all of the following, *except***
    a. 35-mm slides.
    b. A movie.
    c. An on-screen presentation.
    d. Outline pages.

17. **The buttons you use to switch between the PowerPoint views are called**
    a. PowerPoint buttons.
    b. View buttons.
    c. Screen buttons.
    d. Toolbar buttons.

18. **All of the following are PowerPoint views, *except***
    a. Slide view.
    b. Notes Page view.
    c. Outline view.
    d. Current Page view.

19. **The animated character that appears on the screen when you click the Microsoft PowerPoint Help button is the**
    a. Office Helper.
    b. Office Assistant.
    c. Assistant Paper Clip.
    d. PowerPoint Assistant.

20. **The view that allows you to view your electronic slide show with each slide filling the entire screen is called**
    a. Electronic view.
    b. Slide Sorter view.
    c. Presentation view.
    d. Slide Show view.

21. **Which wizard helps you create and outline your presentation?**
    a. Pick a Look Wizard
    b. Presentation Wizard
    c. AutoContent Wizard
    d. OrgContent Wizard

22. **How do you switch to Notes Page view?**
    a. Click the Notes Page View button to the left of the horizontal scroll bar
    b. Click View on the menu bar, then click Notes Page
    c. Press [Shift] and click in the Notes pane
    d. All of the above

PowerPoint 2000

23. How do you save changes to your presentation after you have saved it for the first time?
    a. Click Save As on the File menu, select a filename from the list, then assign it a new name
    b. Click the Save button on the Standard toolbar
    c. Click Save As on the File menu, then click Save
    d. Click Save As on the File menu, specify a new location and filename, then click Save

▶ Skills Review

1. Start PowerPoint and use the AutoContent Wizard.
    a. Start the PowerPoint program, selecting the AutoContent Wizard option.
    b. In the AutoContent Wizard, select a presentation category and type. (*Hint:* If you see a message saying you need to install the feature, insert your Office 2000 CD in the appropriate drive and click OK. See your technical support person for assistance.)
    c. Select the output options of your choice.
    d. Enter appropriate information for the opening slide, enter your name as the footer text, and complete the wizard to show the first slide of the presentation.

2. View the PowerPoint window.
    a. Identify as many elements of the PowerPoint window as you can without referring to the unit material.
    b. For any elements you cannot identify, refer to the unit.

3. View a presentation.
    a. View each slide in the presentation to become familiar with its content.
    b. When you are finished, return to slide 1.
    c. Change to Outline view and review the presentation contents.
    d. Change to Notes Page view and see if the notes pages in the presentation contain text, then return to slide 1.
    e. Examine the presentation contents in Slide Sorter view.
    f. View all the slides of the presentation in Slide Show view, and end the slide show to return to Slide Sorter view.

4. Save a presentation.
    a. Change to the view in which you would like to save your presentation.
    b. Open the Save As dialog box.
    c. Make sure your Project Disk is in the correct drive.
    d. Save your presentation as "Practice."
    e. Embed the fonts in your presentation.
    f. Save your changes to the file.
    g. Go to a different view than the one you saved your presentation in.
    h. Save the changed presentation.

5. **Get Help.**
   a. If the Office Assistant is open, click it. If it is not on your screen, open it.
   b. In the text box, type "Tell me about Help" and click Search.
   c. Select the topic, "Display tips and messages through the Office Assistant."
   d. Click the Show button to open the Help window containing the Contents, Answer Wizard, and Index tabs.
   e. On the Contents tab, double-click any book icon to view the Help subjects (identified by page icons), then click the page icons to review the Help information. Explore a number of topics that interest you.
   f. When you have finished exploring the Contents tab, switch to the Index tab.
   g. In the Type keywords text box, type a word you want help with.
   h. Click a word in the list in box 2 if it did not jump to the correct word, then click Search.
   i. Click a topic in the list in box 3 and read about it.
   j. Explore a number of topics that interest you.
   k. When you have finished exploring the Index tab, close the Help window and hide the Office Assistant.

6. **Print and close the file, and exit PowerPoint.**
   a. Print slides 2 and 3 as slides in grayscale. (*Hint:* In the Slides text box, type 2-3.)
   b. Print all the slides as handouts, 6 slides per page, in pure black and white.
   c. Print all the slides in Outline view.
   d. Resize the slides for overhead transparencies then print slides 1 and 2 in grayscale.
   e. Close the file, saving your changes.
   f. Exit PowerPoint.

▶ Independent Challenges

1. You have just gotten a job as a marketing assistant at Events, Inc., a catering firm specializing in clambakes and barbecues for large company events. John Hudspeth, the marketing manager, has some familiarity with PowerPoint. He has printed his presentation on a black-and-white printer, but he cannot see all of his text, and he wants to know how to solve this problem.

To complete this independent challenge:

a. If PowerPoint is not already running, start it. When the startup dialog box opens, click Cancel. If PowerPoint is already running, go to step b.
b. Use PowerPoint Help to find the answer to John's question.
c. Write down which Help feature you used (Office Assistant, Index, etc.) and the steps you followed.
d. Print the Help window that shows the information you found. (*Hint:* Click the Print button at the top of the Help window.)
e. Exit PowerPoint.

2. You are in charge of marketing for ArtWorks, Inc, a medium-size start-up company that produces all types of art for corporations to enhance their work environment. The company has a regional sales area that includes three neighboring northeastern states. The president of ArtWorks has asked you to plan and create the outline of the PowerPoint presentation he will use to convey his marketing plan to the sales department.

To complete this independent challenge:

a. If necessary, start PowerPoint and choose the AutoContent Wizard option button. (*Hint:* If PowerPoint is already running, click File, click New, click the General tab, and double-click AutoContent Wizard.)

b. Choose the Sales/Marketing category, then choose Marketing Plan from the list.

c. Assign the presentation an appropriate title, and include your name as the footer text.

d. Scroll through the outline the AutoContent Wizard produces. Does it contain the type of information you thought it would?

e. Plan and take notes on how you would change and add to the sample text created by the wizard. What information do you need to promote ArtWorks to companies?

f. Switch views. Run through the slide show at least once.

g. Save your presentation to your Project Disk with the name "ArtWorks."

h. Print your presentation as Handouts (6 slides per page).

i. Close and exit PowerPoint.

3. You have recently been promoted to sales manager at Buconjic Industries. Part of your job is to train sales representatives to go to potential customers and give presentations describing your company's products. Your boss wants you to find an appropriate PowerPoint presentation template that you can use for your next training presentation to recommend strategies to the sales representatives for closing sales. She wants a printout so she can evaluate it.

To complete this independent challenge:

a. If necessary, start PowerPoint and choose the AutoContent Wizard option. (*Hint:* If PowerPoint is already running, click File on the menu bar, click New, click the General tab, and double-click the AutoContent Wizard.)

b. Examine the available AutoContent Wizards and select one that you could adapt for your presentation. (*Hint:* If you see a message saying you need to install additional templates, insert your Office 2000 CD in the appropriate drive and click OK. If you are working in a networked computer lab, see your technical support person for assistance.)

c. Enter an appropriate slide title and your name as the footer text.

d. Print the presentation as an outline, then print the first slide in pure black and white.

e. Write a brief memo to your boss describing which wizard you think will be most helpful, referring to specific slides in the outline to support your recommendations.

f. Save the presentation as "Sales Training" and exit PowerPoint.

4. MediaLoft offers several health care plans to its employees. One of them is AllCare, a health maintenance organization in Memphis, Tennessee. AllCare is offering a new health plan that they would like to present to MediaLoft employees. The director of human resources, Karen Rosen, has heard that you can use PowerPoint 2000 to place presentations on the Internet as Web pages. Because MediaLoft employees are at different locations around the country, Karen is considering putting a PowerPoint presentation on the MediaLoft intranet site to inform employees about the new plan. An intranet is a group of connected networks owned by a company or organization that is used for internal purposes. Intranets use Internet software to handle the data communications, such as e-mail and web pages, within an organization. These pages often provide company-wide information. As with all intranets, the MediaLoft intranet limits access to MediaLoft employees. However, Karen is not sure how this PowerPoint feature works and she would like you to learn about it and give her a brief overview of the subject at the next departmental meeting.

You decide to learn the basics from the PowerPoint Help system, then explore the MediaLoft intranet site yourself to get a better feel for the subject. Then you will be better able to discuss the topic at the meeting.

To complete this independent challenge:

a. If necessary, start PowerPoint and use the Office Assistant Search feature. Type the words "Opening a presentation on the Internet" in the Office Assistant dialog box.

b. When the Assistant displays a list of topics, select the topic, "Open a file on a Web server by using PowerPoint." Read the information in the Help window.

c. Connect to the Internet, go to the MediaLoft intranet site at http://www.course.com/illustrated/MediaLoft.

d. Click each link on the MediaLoft page to become more familiar with the company.

e. Click the Human Resources link, where you will find a presentation about MediaLoft's current health plans. This presentation has been saved in HTML format so that it is a Web page you can view with your browser. Click the MediaLoft Health Plan Options link to start the presentation, then click at the bottom of each slide to move through the presentation. Click the Back button in your browser window to return to the Human Resources page.

f. Disconnect from the Internet, and write a brief memo to Karen explaining how placing presentations on the intranet site will help her communicate the AllCare plan to MediaLoft employees. Attach any Web page printouts that support your recommendations. Include any other options you may have learned about.

g. Exit PowerPoint.

▶ Visual Workshop

Create the presentation shown in Figure A-16 using the Business Plan AutoContent Wizard in the Corporate category. Save the presentation as "Web Plan" on your Project Disk. Print the slides as handouts, six slides per page, in black and white.

FIGURE A-16

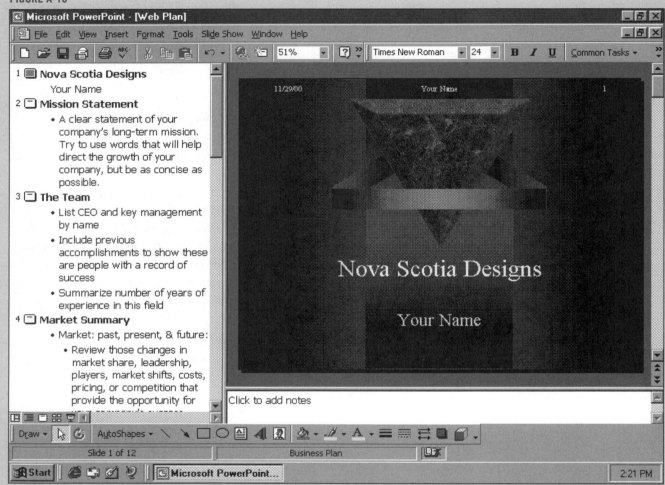

Creating
a Presentation

Objectives

► **Plan an effective presentation**

MOUS ► **Choose a look for a presentation**

MOUS ► **Enter slide text**

MOUS ► **Create a new slide**

MOUS ► **Work in Outline view**

MOUS ► **Enter notes**

MOUS ► **Check spelling in the presentation**

MOUS ► **Evaluate a presentation**

Now that you are familiar with PowerPoint basics, you are ready to plan and create your own presentation. To do this, you enter and edit text and choose a slide design. PowerPoint helps you accomplish these tasks with the AutoContent Wizard and with a collection of professionally prepared slide designs, called **design templates**, which can enhance the look of your presentation. In this unit, you create a presentation using a design template. ✐ Maria Abbott needs to prepare a presentation on MediaLoft's sales for the upcoming annual meeting for store managers. She begins by planning her presentation.

Planning an Effective Presentation

Before you create a presentation using PowerPoint, you need to plan and outline the message you want to communicate and consider how you want the presentation to look. When preparing the outline, you need to consider where you are giving the presentation and who your audience will be. It is also important to know what resources you might need, such as a computer or projection equipment. Using Figure B-1 and the planning guidelines below, follow Maria as she outlines the presentation message.

In planning a presentation it is important to:

 Determine the purpose of the presentation, the location, and the audience
Maria needs to present the highlights of MediaLoft's 1999 sales at the yearly company meeting for store managers in a large room at a business center.

 Determine the type of output—black-and-white or color overhead transparencies, on-screen slide show, or 35-mm slides—that best conveys your message, given time constraints and computer hardware availability
Because Maria is speaking in a large room and has access to a computer and projection equipment, an on-screen slide show is the best choice.

 Determine a look for your presentation that will help communicate your message
You can choose one of the professionally designed templates that come with PowerPoint, modify one of these templates, or create one of your own. Maria wants to establish an upbeat, friendly relationship with the store managers, so she will choose an artistic template.

 Determine the message you want to communicate, then give the presentation a meaningful title and outline your message
Maria wants to highlight the previous year's accomplishments. See Figure B-1.

 Determine what additional materials will be useful in the presentation
You need to prepare not only the slides themselves but supplementary materials, including speaker notes and handouts for the audience. Speaker notes will allow Maria to stay on track and deliver a concise message.

1. Media Loft
    - -1999 Sales Report to Managers
    - -Maria Abbott
    - -General Sales Manager
    - -January 26, 2000
2. 1999: A Banner Year
    - -Overall sales set new record
    - -3 new locations
    - -Book sales post biggest increase
    - -CDs and videos close behind
    - -Café sales steady
3. 1999 Sales by Division
    - -Overall product sales up 22%
    - -MediaLoft East sales up 25%
    - -MediaLoft West sales up 21%
4. The Star: MediaLoft East
    - -Book sales up 29%
    - -CD sales up 25%
    - -Video sales up 20%

Choosing a Look for a Presentation

To help you design your presentation, PowerPoint provides 44 design templates so you don't have to spend time creating the right presentation look. A **design template** has borders, colors, text attributes, and other elements arranged in a specific format that you can apply to all the slides in your presentation. You can use a design template as is, or you can modify any element to suit your needs. Unless you know something about graphic design, it is often easier and faster to use or modify one of the templates supplied with PowerPoint. No matter how you create your presentation, you can save it as a template for future use. ✎ Maria doesn't have a lot of time but wants to create a good-looking presentation, so she uses an existing PowerPoint template.

1. Start PowerPoint, click the **Design Template option button** in the PowerPoint startup dialog box, then click **OK**

   The New Presentation dialog box opens, containing three tabs. See Table B-1 for an overview of the tabs.

2. Click the **Design Templates tab**

   This lists the 44 PowerPoint design templates.

3. Click the **right scroll arrow** if necessary, then click the **Sumi Painting icon** once

   A miniature version of the selected template appears in the Preview box on the right side of the dialog box, as shown in Figure B-2.

4. Click **OK**

   The New Slide dialog box opens, showing 24 AutoLayouts. An **AutoLayout** is a slide containing placeholders for text and graphics. The first AutoLayout is selected, and its name, Title Slide, appears on the right side of the dialog box. Because the first slide of the presentation is the title slide, this layout is appropriate.

5. Click **OK**

   A blank title slide, containing placeholders for title and subtitle text, appears in the Slide pane. The background of the slide and the graphics are part of the Sumi Painting design template you chose. Notice that the name of the template is in the status bar. Notice also that there is a slide icon for slide 1 in the Outline pane.

6. Click **Window** on the menu bar, then click **Arrange All**

   This step adjusts your presentation window so it matches the figures in this book. Compare your screen to Figure B-3.

7. Click **Tools** on the menu bar, click **Customize**, click the **Options tab** in the Customize dialog box, click **Reset my usage data** to restore your toolbars to the default settings, click **Yes**, then click **Close**

8. Click the **Save button** 🖫 on the Standard toolbar, then save your presentation as **1999 Sales Report** to your Project Disk

TABLE B-1: New Presentation dialog box tabs

tab	contains	use
General	A blank presentation and the AutoContent Wizard	To create a presentation from scratch, or to use one of 24 preformatted presentations with suggested content
Design Templates	44 design templates with backgrounds and text formats	To create a presentation with a predesigned template that contains text and graphic designs that coordinate well with each other
Presentations	24 design templates that contain suggested content for specific uses	To create a presentation based on suggested content

FIGURE B-2: **Design Templates tab in the New Presentation dialog box**

Sumi Painting template selected

PowerPoint design templates available

Miniature version of selected template

FIGURE B-3: **Title slide with template design**

Your toolbars may differ

Text placeholders

Sumi Painting template determines background and text arrangement

Name of template

Applying a design template to an existing presentation

You can apply a design template to a presentation at any time. Open the presentation to which you want to apply the template. Click the Common Tasks menu button on the Formatting toolbar, then click Apply Design Template on the drop-down menu. You can also select Apply Design Template on the Format menu. The Apply Design Template dialog box opens with the Presentations Designs folder open. This list of templates is similar to the list that appears on the Design Templates tab in the New Presentation dialog box. Select the template you want to apply. A preview appears in the preview box on the right. Then click Apply. The Apply Design Template dialog box closes and the slide text and background now reflect the template you chose.

PowerPoint 2000

Entering Slide Text

Now that you have applied a template to your new presentation, you are ready to enter text into the title slide. The title slide has two **text placeholders**, boxes with dashed line borders where you enter text. The first text placeholder on the title slide is the **title placeholder** labeled "Click to add title." The second text placeholder on the title slide is the **main text placeholder** labeled "Click to add subtitle." To enter text in a placeholder, simply click the placeholder and then type your text. After you enter text in a placeholder, the placeholder becomes a text object. An **object** is any item on a slide that can be manipulated. Objects are the building blocks that make up a presentation slide. ✒ Maria begins working on her presentation by entering the title of the presentation in the title placeholder.

1. **Move the pointer over the title placeholder labeled "Click to add title" in the Slide pane**
   The pointer changes to I when you move the pointer over the placeholder. In PowerPoint, the pointer often changes shape, depending on the task you are trying to accomplish. Table B-2 describes the functions of the most common PowerPoint mouse pointer shapes.

2. **Click the title placeholder**
   The **insertion point**, a blinking vertical line, indicates where your text will appear in the title placeholder. A **selection box**, the slanted line border, appears around the title placeholder, indicating that it is selected and ready to accept text. See Figure B-4.

3. **Type MediaLoft**
   In the Slide pane, PowerPoint center-aligns the title text within the title placeholder, which is now a text object. Notice that the text appeared in the Ouline pane as you typed.

   > **Trouble?**
   > If you press a wrong key, press [Backspace] to erase the character, then continue to type.

4. **Click the main text placeholder in the Slide pane**
   A wavy, red line may appear under the word "MediaLoft" in the title object indicating that the automatic spellchecking feature in PowerPoint is active. Don't worry if it doesn't appear on your screen.

5. **Type 1999 Sales Report to Managers, then press [Enter]**
   In the Outline pane, this text appears indented under the slide title.

6. **Type Maria Abbott, press [Enter], type General Sales Manager, press [Enter], then type January 26, 2000**
   Compare your title slide to Figure B-5.

7. **Click outside the main text object in a blank area of the slide**
   Clicking a blank area of the slide deselects all selected objects on the slide.

8. **Click the Save button 🖬 on the Standard toolbar to save your changes**

Selection box

Main text placeholder

Title placeholder

Insertion point

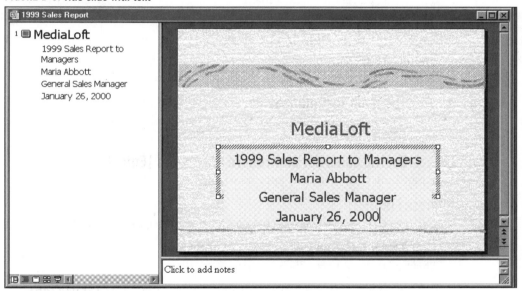

TABLE B-2: **PowerPoint mouse pointer shapes**

shape	description
⩔	Appears when you select the Selection tool; use this pointer to select one or more PowerPoint objects
I	Appears when you move the pointer over a text object; use this pointer, called the I-beam, to place the insertion point where you want to begin typing or selecting text
⟷	Appears when you move the pointer over a bullet, slide icon, or object; use this pointer to select title or paragraph text
+	Appears when you select a drawing tool; use this pointer, called the cross-hair cursor, to draw shapes

PowerPoint 2000

Creating a New Slide

To help you create a new slide easily, PowerPoint offers 24 predesigned AutoLayouts, which include a variety of placeholder arrangements for objects including titles, main text, clip art, graphs, charts, and media clips. You have already used the title slide AutoLayout. Table B-3 describes the different placeholders you'll find in the AutoLayouts. To continue developing the presentation, Maria needs to create a slide that states the main theme of her presentation.

1. Click the **New Slide button** on the Standard toolbar

The New Slide dialog box opens, showing the different AutoLayouts. (Click the down scroll arrow to view more.) This is the same dialog box from which you chose the title slide layout. The title for the selected AutoLayout appears in a Preview box to the right of the layouts, as shown in Figure B-6. You can choose a layout by clicking it. The Bulleted List AutoLayout is already selected.

2. Click **OK**

A new slide appears after the current slide in your presentation. In the Slide pane, it contains a title placeholder and a main text placeholder for the bulleted list. Notice that the status bar indicates Slide 2 of 2. A new slide icon for slide 2 appears in the Outline pane.

3. Click next to the **slide icon** ☐ for slide 2 in the Outline pane, then type **1999: A Banner Year**

As you type, the text appears in the Slide pane also.

4. Click the **main text placeholder** in the Slide pane

You can type text in either pane. The insertion point appears next to a bullet in the main text placeholder.

5. Type **Overall sales set new record**, then press **[Enter]**

A new bullet automatically appears when you press [Enter].

6. Press **[Tab]**

The new first-level bullet indents and becomes a second-level bullet.

7. Type **3 new locations**, then press **[Enter]**

This bullet should actually be a first-level bullet.

8. Click to the left of the **3** that you just typed, then press **[Shift][Tab]**

The item changes back to a first-level bullet.

9. Click after the word **locations**, press **[Enter]**, then enter the next three bulleted items as shown in Figure B-7

10. Click the **Save button** on the Standard toolbar

Your changes are saved to your Project Disk.

FIGURE B-6: New Slide dialog box

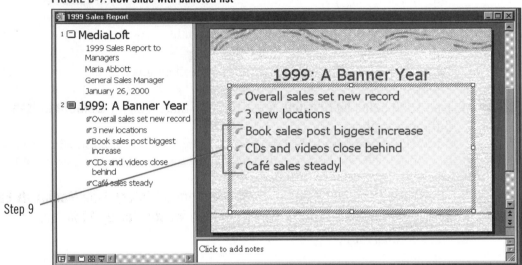

Default AutoLayout

Title of selected layout

FIGURE B-7: New slide with bulleted list

Step 9

TABLE B-3: AutoLayout placeholder types

placeholder	symbol	description
Bulleted List		Inserts a short list of related points
Clip Art		Inserts a picture from the Clip Gallery
Chart		Inserts a chart created with Microsoft Graph
Organization Chart		Inserts an organizational chart
Table		Inserts a table
Media Clip		Inserts a music, sound, or video clip
Object		Inserts an external object such as WordArt, an equation, a spreadsheet, or a picture

Working in Outline View

As you have learned, you can enter your presentation text in the Slide or Outline pane in Normal view. You can also enter text in Slide or Outline view. If you want to focus on the presentation text without worrying about how it looks, Outline view can be a good choice. As in a regular outline, the headings, or **titles**, appear first; then under them, the subpoints, or **main text**, appear. The main text appears as one or more lines of bulleted text indented under a title. Maria switches to Outline view to enter text for two more slides.

QuickTip

You can work in the Outline pane in Normal view if you prefer.

1. Click the **Outline View button** 🔲 to the left of the horizontal scroll bar

   Switching to Outline view enlarges the Outline pane; the Slide and Notes panes become smaller and move to the right side of the screen. The blinking insertion point is in the title of slide 2 (the slide you just created). The Outlining toolbar appears on the left side of the screen.

2. Click anywhere in the last text bullet, press **[Shift]**, then click the **New Slide button** 🔲 on the Standard toolbar

   Pressing [Shift] while clicking 🔲 inserts a new slide with the same AutoLayout as the current slide. A slide icon ⬜ appears next to the slide number when you add a new slide to the outline. See Figure B-8. Text you enter next to a slide icon becomes the title for that slide. The Outlining toolbar is helpful when working in Outline view.

3. Right-click any toolbar, then click **Outlining**

   Table B-4 describes the buttons available on the Outlining toolbar. Because the third slide is a bulleted list like the second slide, you can insert a new slide with the same layout as Slide 2.

Trouble?

If the Outlining toolbar is not visible, click View on the menu bar, point to Toolbars, then click Outlining.

4. Type **1999 Sales by Division**, press **[Enter]**, then click the **Demote button** ➡ on the Outlining toolbar

   A new slide was inserted when you pressed [Enter], but because you want to enter the main text for the slide you just created, you indented this line to make it part of slide 3. You can also press [Tab] to indent text one level.

5. Type **Overall product sales up 22%**, then press **[Enter]**; type **MediaLoft East sales up 25%**, then press **[Enter]**; type **MediaLoft West sales up 21%**, then press **[Enter]**

6. Press **[Shift][Tab]**

   The bullet changes to a new slide icon.

7. Type **The Star: MediaLoft East**, press **[Ctrl][Enter]**, type **Book sales up 29%**, press **[Enter]**, type **CD sales up 25%**, press **[Enter]**, then type **Video sales up 20%**

   Pressing [Ctrl][Enter] while the cursor is in title text creates a bullet. Pressing [Ctrl][Enter] while the cursor is in the main text creates a new slide with the same layout as the previous slide. Two of the bulleted points you just typed for slide 4 are out of order.

8. Position the pointer to the left of the last bullet in slide 4, then click

   The pointer changes from I to ⬌. PowerPoint selects the entire line of text.

QuickTip

You can also drag slide icons or bullets to a new location.

9. Click the **Move Up button** 🔼 on the Outlining toolbar

   The third bullet point moves up one line and trades places with the second bullet point, as shown in Figure B-9.

10. Right-click any toolbar, click **Outlining** to close the Outlining toolbar, click the **Normal View button** 🔲, click the **Previous Slide button** 🔺 below the vertical scroll bar in the Slide pane three times to view each slide, then save your work

    When you are finished viewing all the slides, Slide 1 of 4 should appear in the status bar.

FIGURE B-8: Outline view

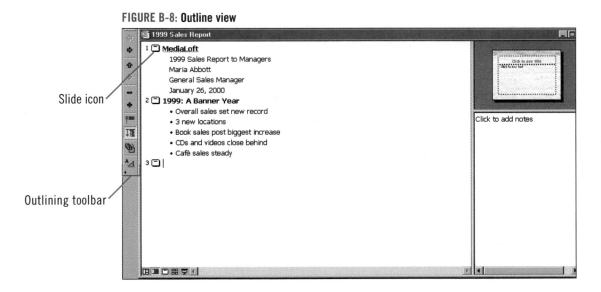

Slide icon

Outlining toolbar

FIGURE B-9: Bulleted item moved up in Outline view

Demote button

Move Up button

Third bullet moved up   Main text   Slide title

TABLE B-4: Outlining toolbar commands

button	button name	description
⬅	**Promote**	Indents selected text one tab to the left
➡	**Demote**	Indents selected text one tab to the right
⬆	**Move Up**	Moves the selection above the previous line
⬇	**Move Down**	Moves the selection below the next line
—	**Collapse**	Shows only the titles of the selected slide
✚	**Expand**	Shows all levels of the selected slide
⏍	**Collapse All**	Shows only the titles of all slides
⏍	**Expand All**	Shows all levels of all slides
⏍	**Summary Slide**	Creates a new bulleted slide containing only the titles of selected slides; good for creating an agenda slide
⏍	**Show Formatting**	Shows or hides all character formatting

Entering Notes

So you don't have to rely on your memory when you give your presentation in front of a group, you can create notes that accompany your slides. You can enter notes in either the Notes pane or in Notes Page view. The notes you enter do not appear on the slides themselves; they are private notes. You can print these pages and refer to them during your presentation. If you want to provide pages on which your audience can take notes, print the notes pages, but leave the text placeholder blank. You can also insert graphics on the notes pages if you use Notes Page view. ✐ To make sure she doesn't forget how she will present the slide information, Maria enters notes to her slides.

Steps 1234

1. **Click in the Notes pane**
   The placeholder text in the Notes pane disappears and the blinking insertion point appears, as shown in Figure B-10.

Trouble?

If you don't see a red, wavy line under the words "MediaLoft" and "Welcom," don't worry. Someone else may have turned this feature off on your machine.

2. **Type Welcom to MediaLoft's Year 2000 company meeting.**
   Make sure you typed "Welcome" without the "e" as shown. The red, wavy line under the words "MediaLoft" and "Welcom" means that these words are not in the Microsoft Office dictionary.

3. **Click the Next Slide button ⬇, click in the Notes pane, then type I'm happy to share with you a brief overview of the success MediaLoft has achieved in the last year.**
   As you type, text automatically wraps to the next line.

4. **Click ⬇ to go to the third slide, click the Notes pane, then type Due to our record year in 1998, MediaLoft's 1999 goals were very aggressive. Our overall product sales were up an amazing 22%, with the eastern division edging out the western division. Of course, they did get 2 of the 3 new stores, so they had an advantage there.**

Trouble?

If you don't see Notes Page on the View menu, point to the double arrow at the bottom of the menu. If you don't see the Zoom list arrow, click the More Buttons button ⁑ on the Standard toolbar.

5. **Click View on the menu bar, click Notes Page, click the Zoom list arrow on the Standard toolbar, then click 100%**
   Because the note on slide 3 is so long, it is easier to read in Notes Page view. See Figure B-11.

6. **Click ⬇, click in the notes placeholder, then type As you can see, the book sales for MediaLoft East were remarkable. We had been concerned about the growth of online booksellers, but there appears to be no substitute for actually holding a book and sipping a cup of cappuccino.**

7. **Press [Enter], then type Thank you all for your hard work and support, and I look forward to working with you all in the new millennium!**

QuickTip

You can also increase the size of the Notes pane in Normal view by dragging the separator line between the Notes pane and the Slide pane.

8. **Click the Normal View button 🔲, then drag the scroll box in the Slide pane vertical scroll bar all the way to the top to return to slide 1**

FIGURE B-10: Insertion point in the Notes pane

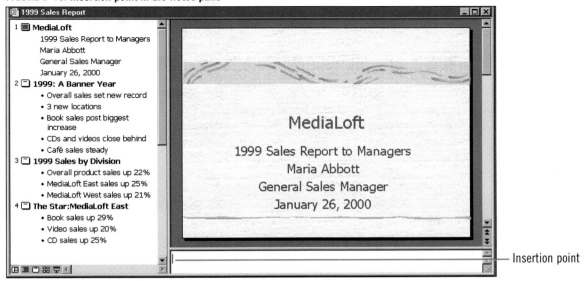

Insertion point

FIGURE B-11: Slide 3 in Notes Page view

Speaker notes

PowerPoint 2000

Adding slide footers and headers

To customize your slides, notes pages, or handouts with information, such as your company or product name, the slide number, or the date, you can add headers and footers. To add a header or footer, click View on the menu bar, then click Header and Footer. Each checked element in the Header and Footer dialog box is included as part of the header or footer. Each check box corresponds to a different footer area. The date and time appear in the left footer area. The slide number appears in the right footer area, and any footer text you add appears in the middle. Click the check boxes and watch to see in which of the three footer areas the footer element appears. On the Slide tab, you can add only footers. To have the footer appear on only the current slide, click Apply; to have footers appear on all the slides, click Apply to All. On the Notes and Handouts tab, you can choose to add headers and footers, so they appear on all the pages.

Checking Spelling in the Presentation

As your work nears completion, you need to review and proofread your presentation thoroughly for errors. You can use the spellchecking feature in PowerPoint to check for and correct spelling errors. The spellchecking feature compares the spelling of all the words in your presentation against the words contained in its electronic dictionary. You still must proofread your presentation for punctuation, grammar, and word-usage errors, however. The spellchecker recognizes only misspelled words, not misused words. For example, the spellchecker would not identify "The Test" as an error even if you had intended to type "The Best." ▰▰▰▰ Maria has finished adding and changing text in the presentation, so she checks her work.

1. **Click the Spelling button [icon] on the Standard toolbar**
   PowerPoint begins to check the spelling in your entire presentation. When PowerPoint finds a misspelled word or a word it doesn't recognize, the Spelling dialog box opens, as shown in Figure B-12. For an explanation of the commands available in the Spelling dialog box, see Table B-5. In this case, PowerPoint does not recognize "MediaLoft" on slide 1. It suggests that you replace it with two separate words "Media" and "Loft," which it does recognize. You want the word to remain as you typed it.

2. **Click Ignore all**
   Clicking Ignore All tells the spellchecker to ignore all instances of this word in this presentation. The next word the spellchecker identifies as an error is the word "Welcom" on the notes for slide 1. In the Suggestions list box, the spellchecker suggests "Welcome."

3. **Click Welcome in the Suggestions list box, then click Change**
   If PowerPoint finds any other words it does not recognize, either change them or ignore them. When the spellchecker finishes checking your presentation, the Spelling dialog box closes, and a PowerPoint alert box opens with a message saying the spelling check is complete.

4. **Click OK**
   The alert box closes.

5. **Click View on the menu bar, then click Header and Footer**
   Before you print your final presentation, placing your name in the footer helps you identify your printout if you are sharing a printer.

6. **On the Slide tab, make sure the Footer check box is selected, click in the Footer text box, then type your name**

7. **Click the Notes and Handouts tab, type your name in the Footer text box, then click Apply to All**
   Now your name will print on slides, notes pages, and handouts.

8. **Click File on the menu bar, then click Print**

9. **Click the Print what list arrow, click Notes Pages, click the Pure black and white check box to select it, click the Frame Slides check box to select it, then click OK**
   The notes pages print with a frame around each page.

10. **Save your presentation, then return to slide 1 in Normal view**

FIGURE B-12: Spelling dialog box

Alternatives appear here

Suggested replacement appears here

Click here to add words to custom dictionary

Click here to leave all occurrences unchanged

Unrecognized word appears here

TABLE B-5: Spelling dialog box commands

command	description
Ignore/Ignore all	Continues spellchecking, without making any changes to the identified word (or all occurrences of the identified word)
Change/Change All	Changes the identified word (or all its occurrences) to the suggested word
Add	Adds the identified word to your custom dictionary; spellchecker will not flag it again
Suggest	Suggests an alternative spelling for the identified word
AutoCorrect	Adds suggested word as an AutoCorrect entry for the highlighted word
Add words to	Lets you choose a custom dictionary where you store words you often use but that are not part of the PowerPoint dictionary

Checking spelling as you type

PowerPoint checks your spelling as you type. If you type a word that is not in the electronic dictionary, a wavy, red line appears under it. To correct the error, right-click the misspelled word. A pop-up menu appears with one or more suggestions. You can select a suggestion, add the word you typed to your custom dictionary, or ignore it. To turn off automatic spellchecking, click Tools on the menu bar, then click Options to open the Options dialog box. Click the Spelling and Style tab, and in the Spelling section click the Check spelling as you type check box to deselect it. To temporarily hide the wavy, red lines, select the Hide spelling errors in this document check box.

Evaluating a Presentation

As you create a presentation, keep in mind that good design involves preparation. An effective presentation is both focused and visually appealing. A planned presentation is easy for the speaker to present and easy for the audience to comprehend. The visual elements (colors, graphics, and text) can strongly influence audience attention and interest and can determine the success of your presentation. Maria evaluates her presentation's effectiveness. Her final presentation is shown in Slide Sorter view in Figure B-13. For contrast, Figure B-14 shows a poorly designed slide.

Steps

1. Click the **Slide Show button** 🖥, then press **[Enter]** to move through the slide show

2. When you are finished viewing the slide show, click the **Slide Sorter View button** ⊞
   Maria decides that slide 4 should come before slide 3.

3. Drag **slide 4** to the left until you see a thin black line between slides 2 and 3, then release the mouse button
   The thin, black line indicates the slide's position.

4. When you are finished evaluating your presentation according to the following guidelines, exit PowerPoint, saving changes when prompted

Details

In evaluating a presentation it is important to:

 Keep your message focused

Don't put everything you are going to say on your presentation slides. Keep the audience anticipating further explanations to the key points shown on your slides. For example, Maria's presentation focuses the audience's attention on last year's sales numbers and sales by division because she included only the sales percentage increases and the breakdown of the sales by division. She supplemented the slides with notes that explain the reasons for the increases.

 Keep the design simple, easy to read, and appropriate for the content

Use appropriate fonts, font sizes, and background colors. A design template makes the presentation consistent. If you design your own layout, do not add so many elements that the slides look cluttered. Use the same design elements consistently throughout the presentation; otherwise, your audience will get confused. The design template Maria used for the sales presentation is simple; the horizontal bar on each slide gives the presentation an interesting, somewhat artistic look, appropriate for a friendly presentation to company employees.

 Choose attractive colors that make the slide easy to read

Use contrasting colors for slide background and text, so that the slides are easy to read. If you are giving your presentation on a computer, you can use almost any combination of colors.

 Keep your text concise

Limit each slide to six words per line and six lines per slide. Use lists and symbols to help prioritize your points visually. Your presentation text provides only the highlights; use notes to give more detailed information.

 Choose fonts and styles that are easy to read and emphasize important text

As a general rule, use no more than two fonts in a presentation and vary font size. Use bold and italic selectively. Do not use text smaller than 18 points. In the design template Maria used, the titles are 44-point Tahoma and the main text is 32-point Tahoma.

 Use visuals to help communicate the message of your presentation

Commonly used visuals include clip art, photographs, charts, worksheets, tables, and movies. Whenever possible, replace text with a visual, but be careful not to overcrowd your slides.

FIGURE B-13: The final presentation

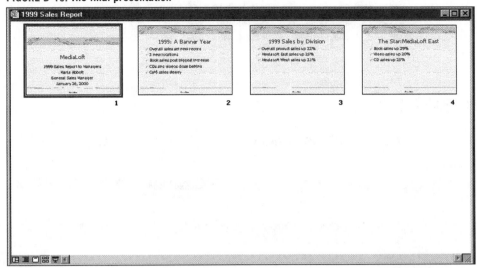

FIGURE B-14: A poorly designed slide in Slide view

Text too small

Graphic obscures text and does not relate to slide message

Too many fonts

Not enough contrast

Too many words

Lines add clutter

Too many colors

Using design templates

You are not limited to the templates in PowerPoint; you can either modify a PowerPoint template or create your own presentation template. For example, you might want to use your company's color as a slide background or incorporate your company's logo on every slide. If you modify an existing template, you can keep, change, or delete any color, graphic, or font. To create a new template, click File on the menu bar, then click New. On the General tab, double-click Blank Presentation, then select the Blank AutoLayout. Add the design elements you want, then use the Save As command on the File menu to name and save your customized design. Click the Save as type list arrow, and choose Design template, then name your template. PowerPoint will automatically add a .pot file extension to the filename. You can then use your customized template as a basis for future presentations. To apply a template from another presentation, open the presentation you want to change, then choose Apply Design Template from the Format menu. In the Apply Design Template dialog box, choose Presentations and Shows in the Files of type list box. Then navigate to and double-click the presentation whose design you want to apply. That presentation's template will be applied to your current presentation.

Practice

► Concepts Review

Label each element of the PowerPoint window shown in Figure B-15.

FIGURE B-15

Match each term with the statement that describes it.

8. Selection box
9. Insertion point
10. Slide icon
11. Design template

a. A specific design, format, and color scheme that is applied to all the slides in a presentation
b. A blinking vertical line that indicates where your text will appear in a text object
c. A box of slanted lines containing prompt text in which you can enter text
d. In Outline view, the symbol that represents a slide

Select the best answer from the list of choices.

12. The ⌶ pointer shape appears for which one of the following tasks?
   a. Entering text
   b Switching views
   c. Choosing a new layout
   d. Inserting a new slide

13. **To move a slide up to a new position in Outline view**
    a. Click ➡
    b. Click ⬆
    c. Press [Tab]
    d. Click ✚

14. **When the spellchecker identifies a word as misspelled, which of the following is not a choice?**
    a. To ignore this occurrence of the error
    b. To change the misspelled word to the correct spelling
    c. To have the spellchecker automatically correct all the errors it finds
    d. To ignore all occurrences of the error in the presentation

15. **When you evaluate your presentation, you should make sure it follows which of the following criteria?**
    a. The slides should include every piece of information to be presented so the audience can read it.
    b. The slides should use as many colors as possible to hold the audience's attention.
    c. Lots of different typefaces will make the slides more interesting.
    d. The message should be clearly outlined without a lot of extra words.

16. **According to the unit, which of the following is *not* a guideline for planning a presentation?**
    a. Determine the purpose of the presentation
    b. Determine what you want to produce when the presentation is finished
    c. Determine which type of output you will need to best convey your message
    d. Determine who else can give the final presentation

17. **Which of the following statements is *not* true?**
    a. You can customize any PowerPoint template.
    b. The spellchecker will identify "there" as misspelled if the correct word for the context is "their."
    c. Speaker notes do not appear during the slide show.
    d. PowerPoint has many colorful templates from which to choose.

18. **Which of the following is *not* a method for changing text levels in the Outline pane or Outline view?**
    a. ⬆
    b. ➖
    c. ⬅
    d. Drag selected text

▶ Skills Review

1. **Choose a look for a presentation.**
    a. Start PowerPoint if necessary and open a new presentation by clicking the Design Template option button or by clicking New on the File menu.
    b. Display the Design Templates tab.
    c. Review the PowerPoint design templates and examine the preview of each one when the template is available.
    d. When you have finished reviewing the templates, open a new presentation using the Mountain template. (*Hint:* If you see a message saying you need to install additional templates, insert the Office 2000 CD in the appropriate drive and click OK. See your technical support person for assistance.)
    e. In the New Slide dialog box, select the Title Slide AutoLayout.
    f. Save the presentation as "Weekly Goals" to your Project Disk.
    g. Go to Slide view and apply the Bold Stripes template from the Design Templates folder.

h. Apply the template from the 1999 Sales Report presentation you created in the unit, and print slides 1 and 2 as Handouts in Grayscale, 6 slides per page.

i. Save the presentation.

2. **Enter slide text.**

   a. In the Slide pane in Normal view or in Slide view, enter the text "Product Marketing" in the title placeholder.

   b. In the main text placeholder, enter "Les Bolinger."

   c. On the next line of the placeholder, enter "Manager."

   d. On the next line of the placeholder, enter "Aug. 2, 2000."

   e. Display and examine the different pointer shapes in PowerPoint. Refer back to Table B-2 to help you display the pointer shapes.

   f. Deselect the text objects.

3. **Create new slides.**

   a. Open the New Slide dialog box, and click each of the AutoLayouts. Identify each AutoLayout by its name in the Preview box.

   b. Select the Bulleted List AutoLayout.

   c. Type "Weekly Meeting for Marketing Groups" in the title placeholder.

   d. Create a new bulleted list slide.

   e. Enter the text from Table B-5 into the new slide.

TABLE B-5

(Slide title)	Goals for the Week
(Main text object, first indent level)	Les
(Main text object, second indent level)	Interview for new marketing rep
	Discuss new procedures with Pacific Rim marketing reps
	Prepare for weekly division meeting next Mon.

4. **Work in Outline view.**

   a. Switch to Outline view

   b. Create a new bulleted list slide after the last one.

   c. Enter the text from Table B-6 into the new slide.

   d. Create a new bulleted list slide after the last one.

   e. Enter the text from Table B-7 into the new slide.

   f. Move slide 5 up to the slide 4 position.

TABLE B-6

(Slide title)	Goals for the Week
(Main text object, first indent level)	John
(Main text object, second indent level)	Revise product marketing report
	Set up plan for the annual sales meeting
	Thurs.—fly to Phoenix for sales meeting planning session

5. **Enter notes.**

   a. Go to slide 3 and place the insertion point in the Notes pane.

   b. Enter the following notes:
   I am interviewing new candidates for the product marketing position.
   The following week, each of you will interview the candidates who meet initial qualifications.
   I need all reports for the weekly meeting by Fri.
   Reminder of the company profit sharing party next Fri. Work half day.
   Open agenda for new division items.

   c. View slide 5.

   d. Enter the following notes:
   I need the marketing report by Wed.
   John: Come by my office later this afternoon to review the sales meeting plan.
   Open agenda for new division items.

TABLE B-7

(Slide title)	Goals for the Week
(Main text object, first indent level)	April
(Main text object, second indent level)	Complete division advertising plan for next year
	Establish preliminary advertising budget for division VP
	Investigate new advertising agencies for company

   e. View slide 4.
   f. Enter the following speaker's notes:
     I need to review the advertising company list by Fri.
     April: See me about weekly division report after this meeting.
     Status on the advertising budget and next year's advertising plan.
     Open agenda for new division items.
   g. Switch to Slide view.

6. Check spelling in the presentation.
   a. Perform a spelling check on the document and change any misspelled words. Ignore any words that are correctly spelled but that the spellchecker doesn't recognize.
   b. Add your name to the footer on all sides and on all notes and handouts.
   c. Add "Product Marketing Presentation" to the left side of the header for Notes and Handouts.
   d. Save the presentation.

7. Evaluate your presentation.
   a. View slide 1 in Slide Show view, then move through the slide show.
   b. Go to Slide Sorter view, then delete slide 2.
   c. Drag slide 4 so that it comes before slide 3.
   d. Evaluate the presentation using the points described in the lesson as criteria.
   e. Print the Notes pages in Pure black and white, with a frame around the page.
   f. Customize the template text by adding the date and time to the left side of the slide footer, then save your new design as a template called Weekly Goals Template.
   g. Print the Notes pages in Grayscale with a frame around the page.

► Independent Challenges

1. You have been asked to give a one-day course at a local adult education center. The course is called "Personal Computing for the Slightly Anxious Beginner" and is intended for adults who have never used a computer. One of your responsibilities is to create presentation slides that outline the course materials.

Plan and create presentation slides that outline the course material for the students. Create slides for the course introduction, course description, course text, grading policies, and a detailed syllabus. For each slide, include speaker notes to help you stay on track during the presentation.

Create your own course material, but assume the following: the school has a computer lab with IBM-compatible computers and Microsoft Windows software; each student has a computer; the prospective students are intimidated by computers but want to learn; and the course is on a Saturday from 9 to 5, with a one-hour lunch break.

To complete this independent challenge:

   a. Think about the results you want to see, the information you need, and the type of message you want to communicate.
   b. Write an outline of your presentation. What content should go on the slides? On the notes pages?
   c. Start PowerPoint and create the presentation by choosing a design template and entering the title slide text.
   d. Create the required slides as well as an ending slide that summarizes your presentation.
   e. Add speaker notes to the slides.
   f. Check the spelling in the presentation.
   g. Save the presentation as "Class 1" to your Project Disk.
   h. View the slide show, then view the slides in Slide Sorter view. Evaluate your presentation, delete any unnecessary slides, and adjust it as necessary so that it is focused, clear, concise, and readable.
   i. Add your name as a footer, then print the slides and notes pages.

2. You are the training director for Events, Inc, a company that coordinates special events, including corporate functions, weddings, and private parties. Events, Inc regularly trains groups of temporary employees that they can call on as coordinators, kitchen and wait staff, and coat checkers for specific events. The company trains 10 to 15 new workers a month for the peak season between May and September. One of your responsibilities is to orient new temporary employees at the next training session.

Plan and create presentation slides that outline your employee orientation. Create slides for the introduction, agenda, company history, dress requirements, principles for interacting successfully with guests, and safety requirements. For each slide, include speaker notes that you can use during the presentation.

Create your own presentation and company material, but assume the following: the new employee training class lasts four hours, and your orientation lasts 15 minutes; the training director's presentation lasts 15 minutes; and the dress code requires uniforms, supplied by Events, Inc (white for daytime events, black and white for evening events).

To complete this independent challenge:

a. Think about the results you want to see, the information you need, and the type of message you want to communicate for this presentation.

b. Write a presentation outline. What content should go on the slides? On the notes pages?

c. Start PowerPoint and create the presentation by choosing a design template, and entering the title slide text.

d. Create an ending slide that summarizes your presentation.

e. Add speaker notes to the slides.

f. Check the spelling in the presentation.

g. Save the presentation as "Training Class" to your Project Disk.

h. View the slide show, then view the slides in Slide Sorter view. Evaluate your presentation, delete any unnecessary slides, and make any changes necessary so that the final version is focused, clear, concise, and readable. Adjust any items as needed.

i. Add your name as a footer, then print the slides and notes pages.

3. You are an independent distributor of natural foods in Tucson, Arizona. Your business, Harvest Natural Foods, has grown progressively since its inception eight years ago, but sales and profits have plateaued over the last nine months. In an effort to stimulate growth, you decide to acquire two major natural food dealers, which would allow Harvest Natural Foods to expand its territory into surrounding states. Use PowerPoint to develop a presentation that you can use to gain a financial backer for the acquisition.

To complete this independent challenge:

a. Start PowerPoint and open a new presentation. Choose the Nature design template. Add "Growth Plan" as the main title on the title slide, and "Harvest Natural Foods" as the subtitle.

b. Save the presentation as "Harvest Proposal" to your Project Disk.

c. Add five more slides with the following titles: slide 2–Background; slide 3–Current Situation; slide 4–Acquisition Goals; slide 5–Our Management Team; slide 6–Funding Required.

d. Enter text into the text placeholders of the slides. Use both Slide and Outline views to enter text.

e. Create a new slide at the end of the presentation. Enter concluding text on the slide, summarizing the main points of the presentation.

f. Add speaker notes that you can use during the presentation.

g. Check the spelling in the presentation.

h. View the presentation as a slide show. Evaluate and save your presentation.

i. Add your name as a footer in the notes and handouts, print the slides as handouts, six per page, and then print the presentation outline.

4. The Literacy Project is a nationwide nonprofit organization that provides free reading and English-language tutoring for adults. Traditionally, the state government has provided most of the funding for the project. However, due to recent state budget cuts, it has become necessary to solicit private corporations and private trusts for grants. MediaLoft has a corporate sponsorship program that works with the Literacy Project. MediaLoft donates books and supplies, encourages interaction between their employees and the program, and helps them raise funds. Karen Rosen, MediaLoft's director of human resources, has appointed you to develop a PowerPoint presentation that the Literacy Project can take to local businesses and trust fund boards to build support. MediaLoft will then loan the Project a portable computer and monitor whenever they need to present the presentation.

The presentation is intended to be a "first contact" with businesses, that will lay the groundwork for a fund-raising proposal at a later date. Therefore, the presentation should educate the corporate audience about the subject of literacy and the need for the Literacy Project, rather than solicit funds directly.

To complete this independent challenge:

a. Connect to the Internet, go to the MediaLoft intranet site at http://www.course.com/illustrated/MediaLoft and click the Community link. Scroll down to and click the Literacy Project link, and read the information it contains.

b. Start PowerPoint, open a new presentation, and apply an appropriate design template, keeping in mind your business audience. Add "Literacy Project" as the main title on the title slide, and add "Improving Tomorrow's Workforce While Building Your Community" as the subtitle.

c. Create a presentation of at least five slides that will educate the corporate audience and convince them of a need for the Literacy Project. Use both Slide and Outline panes or views to enter text.

d. Create a new slide at the end of the presentation. Enter concluding text on the slide, summarizing your main points.

e. Apply a different design template to the presentation. If you don't care for the results, reapply the original design template.

f. Add speaker notes to the slides.

g. Spellcheck the presentation.

h. Save the presentation as "Literacy Presentation" to your Project Disk. Disconnect from the Internet when you are done.

i. View the presentation as a slide show and evaluate your presentation. Delete any unnecessary slides. Save any changes you make.

j. Add you name as a footer, then print the slides as handouts, six per page, and print the outline.

► Visual Workshop

Create the marketing presentation shown in Figures B-16 and B-17. Save the presentation as "Sales Project" to your Project Disk. Review your slides in Slide Show view, add your name as a footer, then print the first slide of your presentation in Slide view and print the outline.

FIGURE B-16

FIGURE B-17

Modifying
a Presentation

Objectives

- MOUS ▶ **Open an existing presentation**
- MOUS ▶ **Draw and modify an object**
- MOUS ▶ **Edit drawing objects**
- ▶ **Understand aligning, grouping, and stacking objects**
- MOUS ▶ **Align and group objects**
- MOUS ▶ **Add and arrange text**
- MOUS ▶ **Format text**
- MOUS ▶ **Customize the color scheme and background**
- ▶ **Correct text automatically**

After you create the basic outline of your presentation and enter text, you need to add visuals to your slides to communicate your message in the most effective way possible. In this unit, you open an existing presentation; draw and modify objects; add, arrange, and format text; change a presentation color scheme; and automatically correct text.
After Maria Abbott reviews her presentation, she continues to work on the Sales Report presentation. Maria uses the PowerPoint drawing and text-editing features to bring the presentation closer to a finished look.

PowerPoint 2000

Opening an Existing Presentation

Sometimes the easiest way to create a new presentation is by changing an existing one. Revising a presentation saves you from typing duplicate information. You simply open the file you want to change, then use the Save As command to save a copy of the file with a new name. Whenever you open an existing presentation in this book, you will save a copy of it with a new name to your Project Disk—this keeps the original file intact. Saving a copy does not affect the original file. Maria wants to add visuals to her presentation, so she opens the presentation she has been working on.

1. Start PowerPoint and insert your Project Disk into the appropriate disk drive

QuickTip

If PowerPoint is already running, click the Open button on the Standard toolbar.

2. Click the **Open an existing presentation option button** in the PowerPoint startup dialog box, click **More Files** in the scrollable window, then click **OK**
   The Open dialog box opens. See Figure C-1.

3. Click the **Look in list arrow**, then locate the drive that contains your Project Disk

4. Click the drive that contains your Project Disk
   A list of the files on your Project Disk appears in the Open dialog box.

Trouble?

If the Open dialog box on your screen does not show a preview box, click the Views list arrow in the toolbar at the top of the dialog box, then select Preview.

5. Click **PPT C-1**
   The first slide of the selected presentation appears in the preview box on the right side of the dialog box.

6. Click **Open**
   The file named PPT C-1 opens in Slide view.

7. Click **File** on the menu bar, then click **Save As**
   The Save As dialog box opens. See Figure C-2. The Save As dialog box works just like the Open dialog box.

QuickTip

When you save copies of files, you may want to use a naming system to help you stay organized and differentiate different versions of a document. Many people use the name of the original file followed by consecutive numbers (1, 2, 3. . .) or letters (a, b, c. . .) to designate revisions of the same document or presentation.

8. Make sure the Save in list box shows the drive containing your Project Disk and that the current filename in the File name text box is selected, then type **1999 Sales Report 1**
   Compare your screen to the Save As dialog box in Figure C-2.

9. Click **Save** to close the Save As dialog box and save the file
   PowerPoint creates a copy of PPT C-1 with the name 1999 Sales Report 1 on your Project Disk and closes PPT C-1.

10. Click **Window** on the menu bar, then click **Arrange All**
   Your screen now matches those shown in this book. If you have another PowerPoint presentation open and it appears next to this presentation, close it, then repeat step 10.

FIGURE C-1: Open dialog box

Step 3

Your list of files may be different

Click here to find files

Step 5

Preview box

Step 6

FIGURE C-2: Save As dialog box

Step 8

Step 9

Searching for a file by properties

If you can't find a file, you can search for it using the PowerPoint Find dialog box, which you open from the Tools menu in the Open dialog box. (See Figure C-1.) To search for a file, open the Open dialog box, click the Tools menu button on the toolbar at the top of the dialog box, then click Find on the drop-down list. The Find dialog box opens. You can specify criteria PowerPoint should use to search by clicking the list arrows in the Property, Condition, and Value boxes at the bottom of the dialog box. A property is any aspect of a presentation, such as its filename, title, contents, size, or format. For example, you can specify that you want to find a presentation whose filename (property) includes (condition) the words "sales presentation" (value). Once you've specified criteria, click Add to List. To specify where PowerPoint should search for the file, click the Look in list arrow and select the drive or folder you want to search. To include subfolders in the search, click the Search subfolders check box to select it. Click Find Now to start the search. PowerPoint closes the Find dialog box and lists the folders and files that meet your criteria in the Look in list box in the Open dialog box.

Drawing and Modifying an Object

The drawing capabilities of PowerPoint allow you to draw and modify lines, shapes, and pictures to enhance your presentation. Lines and shapes that you create with the PowerPoint drawing tools are objects that you can modify and move at any time. These drawn objects have graphic attributes that you can change, such as fill color, line color, line style, shadow, and 3-D effects. To add drawing objects to your slides, use the buttons on the Drawing toolbar at the bottom of the screen above the status bar. ✎ Maria decides to draw an object on slide 4 of her sales report presentation to add impact to her message.

Steps

1. Click **Tools** on the menu bar, click **Customize**, click the **Options tab** in the Customize dialog box, click **Reset my usage data** to restore the default settings, click **Yes** in the alert box or dialog balloon that opens, then click **Close**
   This restores the default settings to your toolbars.

2. In the Outline pane, click the **slide icon** ☐ for slide 4
   The 1999 Sales by Division slide appears.

3. Press and hold **[Shift]**, then click the **main text object**
   A dotted selection box with small boxes called **sizing handles** appears around the text object. If you click a text object without pressing [Shift], a selection box composed of slanted lines appears indicating the object is active, but not selected. When an entire object is selected, you can change its size, shape, or attributes.

   Trouble?
   If you are not satisfied with the size of the text object, resize it again.

4. Position the pointer over the right, middle sizing handle, then drag the sizing handle to the left until the text object is about half its original size
   When you position the pointer over a sizing handle, it changes to ↔. It points in different directions depending on which sizing handle it is positioned over. When you drag a text object's sizing handle, the pointer changes to +, and a dotted outline representing the size of the text object appears. See Figure C-3.

   QuickTip
   Position the pointer on top of a button to see its name.

5. Click the **AutoShapes menu button** on the Drawing toolbar, point to **Stars and Banners**, then click the **Up Ribbon button** 🎀 (third row, first item)
   After you select a shape from the AutoShapes menu and move the pointer over the slide, the pointer changes to +.

   QuickTip
   To create a circle or square, click the Oval or Rectangle button on the Drawing toolbar, then press [Shift] while dragging the pointer.

6. Position + in the blank area of the slide to the right of the text object, press **[Shift]**, drag down and to the right to create a ribbon object, as shown in Figure C-4, then release the mouse button and release **[Shift]**
   When you release the mouse button, a ribbon object appears on the slide, filled with the default color and outlined with the default line style, as shown in Figure C-4. Pressing [Shift] while you create the object keeps the object's proportions as you change its size.

7. If your ribbon object is not approximately the same size as the one shown in Figure C-4, press **[Shift]** and drag one of the sizing handles to resize the object

8. Click the **Line Color list arrow** 🖊▾ on the Drawing toolbar, then click the **light purple square** (the third square from the right, called Follow Accent Scheme Color)
   PowerPoint applies the purple color to the selected object's outline.

9. Click the **Fill Color list arrow** 🎨▾ on the Drawing toolbar, then click the **dark purple square** (the fourth square from the left, called Follow Title Text Scheme Color)
   PowerPoint fills the ribbon with the dark purple color.

FIGURE C-3: Resizing a text object

Step 2 ─────

Dotted outline ─────

Mouse pointer

Sizing handles

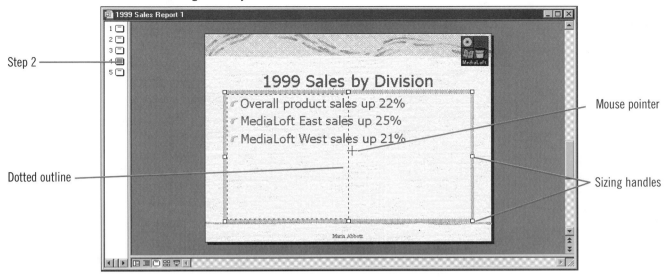

FIGURE C-4: Slide showing ribbon object

Using the Drawing toolbar

The Drawing toolbar contains many useful buttons for drawing and modifying objects on PowerPoint slides (See Figure C-5). You use the buttons on the left, including the Draw menu button, to manipulate objects. When you click the Draw menu button, a menu of commands useful for manipulating objects opens. The buttons in the middle section are used to create objects on your slides. You use the buttons in the far right section to modify objects once they have been created. To find out about a particular button, point to it to see its name in a ScreenTip, or click Help on the menu bar, click What's This, then click the button to see a brief description.

FIGURE C-5: The Drawing toolbar

Editing Drawing Objects

Often, a drawn object does not match the slide or presentation "look" you are trying to achieve. PowerPoint allows you to manipulate the size and shape of objects on your slide. You can alter the appearance of any object by changing its shape, as you did when you resized the text object in the previous lesson, or by adjusting the object's dimensions. You also can cut, copy, and paste objects and add text to most PowerPoint shapes. ➤ Maria changes the shape of the ribbon object, then makes two copies of it to help emphasize each point on the slide.

Steps 1 2 3 4

1. **Click the ribbon object to select it, if necessary**
   In addition to sizing handles, small yellow diamonds called **adjustment handles** appear. You change these handles to change the appearance of an object, usually its most prominent feature, like the size of an arrow head, or the proportion of a ribbon's center to its "tails."

2. **Drag the bottom, right sizing handle to the right about 1"**

Trouble?

If you have trouble aligning the objects with the text, press and hold down [Alt] while dragging the object to turn off the automatic grid.

3. **Position the pointer over the middle of the selected ribbon object so that it changes to ⬚, then drag the ribbon so that the top of the ribbon aligns with the top of the first bullet**
   A dotted outline appears as you move the ribbon object to help you position it. Compare your screen to Figure C-6 and make any necessary adjustments.

4. **Position ⬚ over the ribbon object, then press and hold [Ctrl]**
   The pointer changes to ⬚, indicating that PowerPoint will make a copy of the ribbon object when you drag the mouse.

QuickTip

You can use PowerPoint rulers to help you align objects. To display the rulers, position the pointer in a blank area of the slide, right-click, then click Ruler in the pop-up menu. Or, click View on the menu bar, and then click Ruler.

5. **While holding down [Ctrl], drag the ribbon object down the slide until dotted lines indicate that the copy aligns with the second bullet, then release the mouse button**
   An exact copy of the first ribbon object appears. See Figure C-7.

6. **Position the pointer over the second ribbon object, press and hold [Ctrl], then drag a copy of the ribbon object down the slide until it aligns with the third bullet**
   Compare your screen to Figure C-7.

7. **Click the top ribbon object, then type 22%**
   The text appears in the center of the object. The text is now part of the object, so if you move the object, the text will move with it.

QuickTip

Text entered in an AutoShape appears on one line unless you change it. With the AutoShape selected, click Format on the menu bar, click AutoShape, select the Word wrap text in the AutoShape check box, then click OK.

8. **Click the middle ribbon object, type 25%, then click the bottom ribbon object and type 21%**
   The graphics you have added reinforce the slide text. The ribbon shape suggests achievement, and the numbers, which are the focus of this slide, are prominent. The dark text is hard to read on the dark background.

9. **Press and hold [Shift], click the other two ribbon objects, click the Font Color list arrow A▾ on the Drawing toolbar, then click the white square**
   Make sure the bottom ribbon object is still selected when you select the other two objects. The text changes to white.

10. **Click a blank area of the slide to deselect the objects, then save your presentation**

FIGURE C-6: Slide showing resized ribbon object

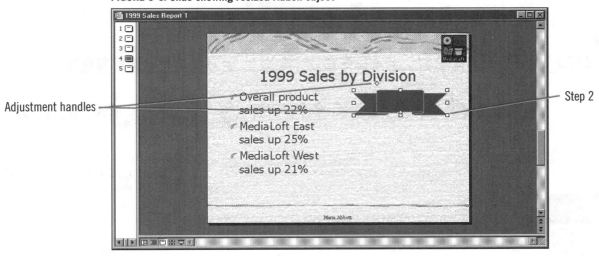

Adjustment handles

Step 2

FIGURE C-7: Slide showing duplicated ribbon object

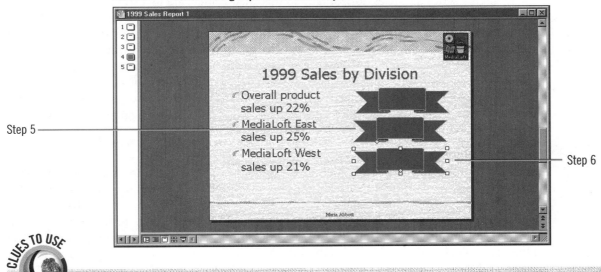

Step 5

Step 6

Using the Office Clipboard

In this lesson, you copied objects using the Ctrl-Drag technique. You can also copy objects using the Office Clipboard, which lets you copy and paste multiple items. You can store up to 12 text or graphic items on the Office Clipboard. See Figure C-8. When you copy a second item within any Office program, the program automatically places the second item on the Office Clipboard. If you put 12 items on the Office Clipboard and then copy a thirteenth item, the program asks you if you want to remove the first item. You can check the contents of a particular item on the Office Clipboard by holding the pointer over it to display a ScreenTip. You can then paste one or more of the items from the Office Clipboard to a slide in your PowerPoint presentation. Just click the item you want to paste on the Clipboard toolbar and PowerPoint inserts it in the presentation. To paste all the items on the Clipboard, click Paste All on the Clipboard toolbar. The items you collect on the Office Clipboard remain there until you quit all Office programs. To clear the Office Clipboard, click Clear Clipboard on the Clipboard toolbar. You can copy and paste items among any of the Office programs.

FIGURE C-8: Clipboard toolbar

MODIFYING A PRESENTATION POWERPOINT C-7

Understanding Aligning, Grouping, and Stacking Objects

As you work in PowerPoint, you often work with multiple objects on the same slide. These may be text objects or graphics objects, such as clip art, drawings, photos, tables, or charts. When you have more than one object on a slide, you want to make sure they look organized and neat and that they help communicate your message effectively. You can accomplish this by aligning, grouping, and stacking the objects using the commands on the Draw menu on the Drawing toolbar.

Aligning objects

When you **align** objects, you place their edges (or their centers) on the same plane. For example, you might align squares vertically so that their left edges are in a straight vertical line. Or you might align a series of circles horizontally so that their centers are in a straight horizontal line. You align objects in PowerPoint by first selecting the objects you want to align. Next, click the Draw menu button on the Drawing toolbar, point to Align or Distribute, then select one of the three horizontal alignment commands (Align Left, Align Center, or Align Right), or one of the three vertical alignment commands (Align Top, Align Middle, or Align Bottom). Aligning saves you time, because you don't have to drag each object individually. The PowerPoint Align commands make your slides look neater and more professional because they can do a better job than most people can do by manually dragging objects with the mouse and aligning them "by eye." See Figure C-9.

Grouping objects

When you **group** objects, you combine two or more objects into one object. For example, instead of having to move four squares, you could group them and then only have to move one object that contains the four squares. It's often helpful to group objects that you have aligned, so that when you move the group, the alignment among the objects remains the same. To group objects on a PowerPoint slide, you first select the objects, click the Draw menu button on the Drawing toolbar, and then click Group. You can easily ungroup objects by clicking a grouped object and then selecting the Ungroup command on the Draw menu. See Figure C-10.

Stacking objects

When you **stack** objects, you determine their order in a stack—that is, which ones are in the front and which are in back. You can easily move objects on top of each other to create effects. For example, you'll often want to place a word on top of a circle or square, or place graphics on top of other graphics. To control the stacking order of objects on a PowerPoint slide, you select the object whose order you want to adjust, click the Draw menu button on the Drawing toolbar, point to Order, and then click one of the four Order commands: Bring to Front, Send to Back, Bring Forward, or Send Backward. See Figure C-11.

FIGURE C-9: Aligning

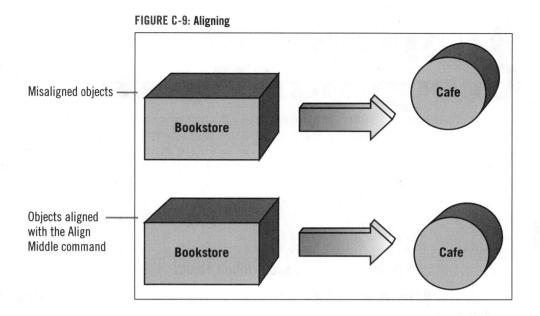

Misaligned objects

Objects aligned with the Align Middle command

FIGURE C-10: Grouping

Two ungrouped objects

One grouped object

FIGURE C-11: Stacking

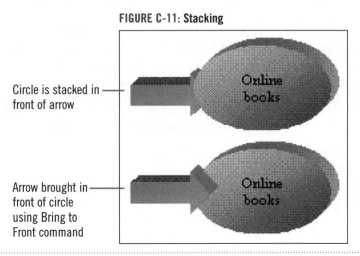

Circle is stacked in front of arrow

Arrow brought in front of circle using Bring to Front command

Aligning and Grouping Objects

After you create objects, modify their appearance, edit their size and shape, and position them on the slide, you can align and group them. The Align command aligns objects relative to each other by snapping the selected objects to an invisible grid of evenly spaced vertical and horizontal lines. The Group command groups objects into one object to make editing and moving them much easier. ▰▰▰▰ Maria aligns, groups, and positions the ribbon objects. Then she copies the grouped ribbon object and pastes it on the next slide.

Steps

1. Press and hold **[Shift]**, then click **each ribbon object** to select all three objects

2. Click the **Draw menu button** on the Drawing toolbar, then point to **Align or Distribute**

   A menu of alignment and distribution options appears. The top three options align objects horizontally; the next three options align objects vertically.

3. Click **Align Center**

   The ribbon objects align on their centers, as shown in Figure C-12.

4. Click the **Draw menu button**, then click **Group**

   The ribbon objects group to form one object without losing their individual attributes. Notice the sizing handles now appear around the outer edge of the grouped object, not around each individual object.

5. Right-click a blank area of the slide, then click **Guides** on the pop-up menu

   The PowerPoint guides appear as gray dotted lines on the slide. (The dotted lines might be very faint on your screen.) The guides intersect at the center of the slide. They will help you position the ribbon object on the slide.

6. Position ▱ over the **vertical guide** in a blank area of the slide, press and hold the mouse button until the pointer changes to a guide measurement box, then drag the guide to the right until the guide measurement box reads approximately **1.75**

7. Press **[Shift]**, drag the grouped ribbon object over the vertical guide until the center sizing handles are approximately centered over the vertical guide

   Pressing [Shift] while you drag an object constrains its movement to vertical or horizontal.

Trouble?

Click the More Buttons button ▱ to locate buttons that are not visible on a toolbar.

8. Right-click the ribbon object, click **Copy** on the pop-up menu, click the **Next Slide button** ▱, then click the **Paste button** ▱ on the Standard toolbar

   Slide 5 appears and the grouped ribbon object from slide 4 is pasted onto slide 5. Notice that the position of the pasted ribbon object on slide 5 is the same as it was on slide 4.

9. Triple-click the **top ribbon object**, type **29%**, triple-click the **middle ribbon object**, type **20%**, triple-click the **bottom ribbon object**, type **25%**, then click in a blank area of the slide

   You do not have to ungroup the objects in order to change the text on them.

10. Click **View** on the menu bar, then click **Guides** to hide the guides

    Compare your screen to Figure C-13.

FIGURE C-12: Aligned ribbon objects

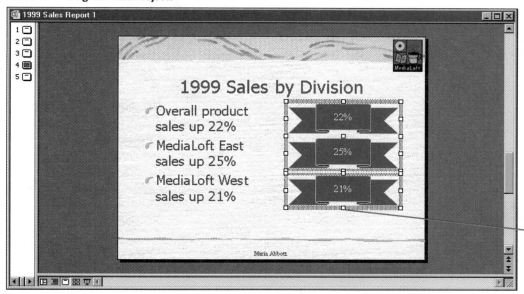

Objects aligned horizontally on their centers

FIGURE C-13: Slide 5 showing pasted ribbon objects

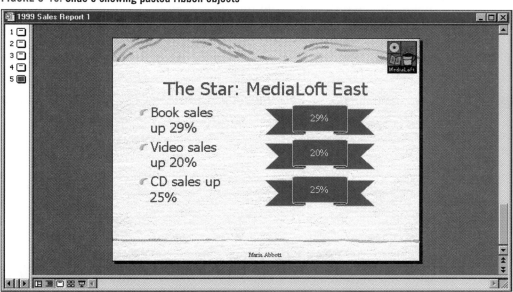

More ways to change objects

You can change the appearance of an object by rotating or flipping it, or by making it three-dimensional. To rotate or flip an object, select it, click the Draw menu button on the Drawing toolbar, point to Rotate or Flip, then click one of the available menu commands, as shown in Figure C-14. Clicking a Flip command creates a mirror image. Clicking a Rotate command turns an object 90°. To make an object three-dimensional, select it, click the 3-D button , and click one of the options shown on the 3-D menu in Figure C-15. To add a shadow to an object, click the Shadow button on the Drawing toolbar, then click one of the buttons on the pop-up menu.

FIGURE C-14: Rotate or Flip submenu   **FIGURE C-15:** 3-D menu

Adding and Arranging Text

Using the advanced text editing capabilities of PowerPoint, you can easily add, insert, or rearrange text. On a PowerPoint slide, you can enter text in prearranged text placeholders. If these text placeholders don't provide the flexibility you need, you can use the Text Box button on the Drawing toolbar to create your own text objects. With the Text Box button, you can create two types of text objects: a text label, used for a small phrase inside a box where text doesn't automatically wrap to the next line, and a word-processing box, used for a sentence or paragraph where the text wraps inside the boundaries of a box. ✎ Maria already added a slide to contain a quote from a recent review. Now, she uses the Text Box button to create a word-processing box on slide 3 in which to enter the quote.

1. Click the **slide icon** ⬚ for slide 3 in the Outline pane

2. Click the **Text Box button** 📧 on the Drawing toolbar

3. Position the pointer about ½" from the left side of the slide and about even with the top of the picture already on the slide, then drag a word-processing box toward the picture so that your screen looks like Figure C-16
After you click 📧, the pointer changes to ↓. When you begin dragging, an outline of the box appears, indicating how wide a text object you are drawing. After you release the mouse button, an insertion point appears inside the text object, ready to accept text.

QuickTip
Notice that after you type the word café and press [Spacebar], the PowerPoint AutoCorrect feature automatically inserts an accent over the e in café.

4. Type **Modeled on the café bookstore, MediaLoft takes the concept to new heights!**, press **[Enter]**, then type **Business Day, August 1999**
Notice that the word-processing box increases in size as your text wraps inside the object. There is a mistake in the quote. It should read "bookstore café" not "café bookstore."

5. Double-click I on the word **bookstore** to select it
When you select a word, the pointer changes from I to ⇧ .

QuickTip
You also can use the Cut and Paste buttons on the Standard toolbar and the Cut and Paste commands on the Edit menu to move a word.

6. Position the pointer on top of the selected word and press and hold the mouse button
The pointer changes to ⇧. A dotted insertion line indicates where PowerPoint will place the word when you release the mouse button.

7. Drag the word **bookstore** to the left of the word **café** in the quote, then release the mouse button

QuickTip
To create a text label in which text doesn't wrap, click 📧, position ↓ where you want to place the text, then click once and enter the text.

8. If necessary, drag the text box to reposition it so that it looks similiar to Figure C-17

9. Click a blank area of the slide outside the text object, then save your changes
The text object is deselected. Your screen should look similar to Figure C-17.

Inserting slides from other presentations

To copy slides, open both presentations in Slide Sorter view, select the desired slides, then paste them into the current presentation. To insert slides, click Insert on the menu bar, then click Slides from Files. Click the Browse button in the Slide Finder dialog box, then locate the presentation from which you want to copy slides. In the Select slides section, select the slide(s) you want to insert, click Insert, then click Close. The new slides automatically take on the design of the current presentation.

FIGURE C-16: Slide showing word-processing box ready to accept text

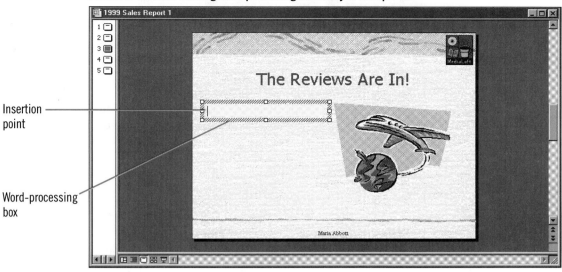

Insertion point

Word-processing box

FIGURE C-17: Slide after adding text to the word-processing box

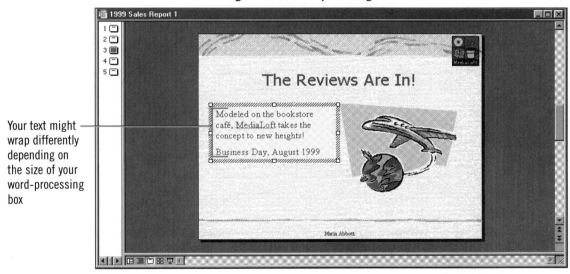

Your text might wrap differently depending on the size of your word-processing box

Importing text from Microsoft Word

You may want to create a presentation on a subject you wrote about earlier using Microsoft Word 2000. You can easily save time creating a presentation by importing the Word outline. You can import an outline to create a new presentation, or you can import an outline into an existing presentation. To create a new presentation from a Word outline, click the Open button ⬚ on the Standard toolbar. Then in the Files of type list box, click All outlines, and double-click the name of the file you want to import. (You may receive a message asking you to insert the Office CD so the program can install a converter.) To insert an outline into an existing presentation, click the slide after which you want to insert the new information in the Outline pane or Outline view. Click Insert on the menu bar, then click Slides from Outline. Make sure the Files of type text box displays All Files, click the name of the file you want to import, then click Insert. When you import a Word outline, PowerPoint automatically creates slides containing the items from your outline, using the Outline level 1 heads as slide titles, and the lower level items as body text on the slides.

Formatting Text

Once you have entered and arranged the text in your presentation, you can change and modify the way the text looks to emphasize your message. Important text needs to be highlighted in some way to distinguish it from other text or objects on the slide. Less important information needs to be deemphasized. For example, if you have two text objects on the same slide, you could draw attention to one text object by changing its color or size. To change the way text looks, you need to select it, and then choose a Formatting command. ✐ Maria uses some of the commands on the Formatting and Drawing toolbars to change the way the review quote looks.

Steps

1. On slide 3, press **[Shift]**, then click the **text box**

If a text box is already active because you have been entering text in it, you can select the entire text box by clicking on its edge with 🖈. The entire text box is selected. Any changes you make will affect all the text in the selected text box. Changing the text's size and appearance will help emphasize it.

Trouble?

Click the More Buttons button ⌗ to locate buttons that are not visible on your toolbar.

2. Click the **Increase Font Size button** 🅰 on the Formatting toolbar twice

Note that after you click 🅰 once, it moves to the Formatting toolbar. The text increases in size to 32 points.

3. Click the **Italic button** 𝐼 on the Formatting toolbar

The text changes from normal to italic text. The Italic button, like the Bold button, is a toggle button, which you click to turn the attribute on or off.

4. Click the **Font Color list arrow** 🄰▾ on the Drawing toolbar

The Font Color menu appears, showing the eight colors used in the current presentation and More Font Colors, which lets you choose additional colors.

5. Click **More Font Colors**, then in the Colors dialog box, click the **Standard tab**

6. In the color hexagon, click the **blue color cell** in the third row from the top, fourth from right, then click **OK**

The Current color and the New color appear in the box in the lower-right corner of the dialog box. The text in the word-processing box changes to the blue color.

7. Click the **Font list arrow** on the Formatting toolbar

A list of available fonts opens, as shown in Figure C-18. A double line at the top of the font list may separate the fonts most recently used from the complete list of available fonts.

8. Click the scroll arrows if necessary, then click **Arial**

The Arial font replaces the original font in the text object.

QuickTip

To automatically wrap text in an AutoShape, drag a text box in the desired width, type your text, then group the two objects.

9. Drag the pointer over the text **Business Day, August 1999**, click the **Font Size list arrow** on the Formatting toolbar, click **18**, then click the **Align right button** 🗏 on the Formatting toolbar

The pointer changes to Ⅰ when you drag it over text. The source text is now smaller and right-aligned. Only the selected text is affected by the formatting command, not the entire text object.

10. Drag the text box to center it vertically, click a blank area of the slide outside the text object to deselect it, then click the **Save button** 🖫 on the Standard toolbar

Compare your screen to Figure C-19.

FIGURE C-18: Font list open

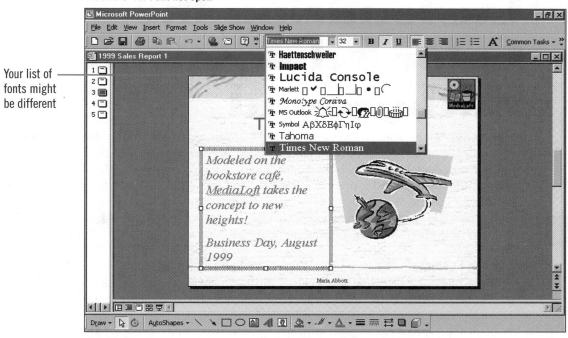

Your list of fonts might be different

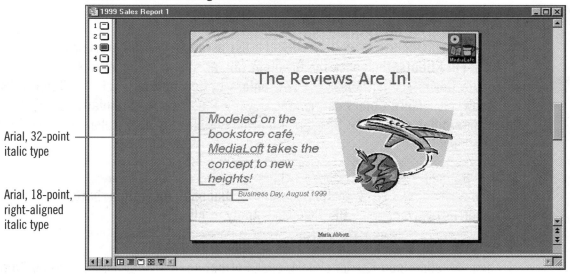

FIGURE C-19: Slide showing formatted text box

Arial, 32-point italic type

Arial, 18-point, right-aligned italic type

Replacing Text and Attributes

As you review your presentation, you may decide to replace certain words or fonts throughout the entire presentation. You can automatically modify words, sentences, fonts, text case, and periods. To replace specific words or sentences, use the Replace command on the Edit menu. To change a font, use the Replace Fonts command on the Format menu. To automatically add or remove periods from title or body text and to automatically change the case of title or body text, click Options on the Tools menu, click the Spelling and Style tab, then click Style Options to open the Style Options dialog box. Click the Case and End Punctuation tab. The options on the Visual Clarity tab in the Style Options dialog box control the legibility of bulleted text items on the slides.

PowerPoint 2000

Customizing the Color Scheme and Background

Every PowerPoint presentation has a set of eight coordinated colors, called a **color scheme**, that determines the main colors for the slide elements in your presentation: slide background, text and lines, title text, shadows, fills, and accents. See Table C-1 for a description of the slide color scheme elements. The **background** is the area behind the text and graphics. Every design template has a default color scheme that you can use, or you can create your own. You can also change the background color and appearance independent of changing the color scheme. ✎ Maria decides she doesn't like the color scheme or the white background, so she decides to change it.

Steps 1 2 3 4

1. Click **Format** on the menu bar, then click **Slide Color Scheme**

   The Color Scheme dialog box opens with the Standard tab active. See Figure C-20. The number of preset color schemes available depends on the elements in the current presentation. The current color scheme is selected with a black border.

QuickTip

To apply a new color scheme to only selected slides, switch to Slide Sorter view, select the slides you want to change, then click Apply instead of Apply to All in the dialog box.

2. Click the second color scheme in the top row, then click **Apply to All**

   The dialog box closes, and the new color scheme is applied to all the slides in the presentation. In this case, the new color scheme changes the color of the slide graphics, but the text and background remain the same.

3. Click **Format** on the menu bar, then click **Background**

   The Background dialog box opens.

4. In the Background fill section, click the **list arrow** below the preview of the slide, click **Fill Effects**, then click the **Gradient tab**, as shown in Figure C-21

QuickTip

Note that if you click the Preset option button, you can choose from a variety of predesigned backgrounds. To add a textured background to a slide, click the Texture tab, select any texture, read its name below the texture icons, click OK, then click Apply or Apply to All.

5. In the Colors section, click the **Two colors option button**, click the **Color 2 list arrow**, click **More Colors** on the drop-down menu, click the **Standard tab**, click the **orange color cell** in the fifth row from the bottom, the sixth color from the right, then click **OK**

   The horizontal shading style is selected, as is the first of the four variants, showing that the background is shaded from color 1 (white) on the top to color 2 (orange) on the bottom.

6. In the Shading Styles section, click the **Diagonal up option button**, click the **upper-left variant**, click **OK**, then click **Apply to All**

   The background is now shaded from white (upper-left) to orange (lower-right). The ribbons on slides 4 and 5 would look better in plum.

7. Click the **slide icon** ▭ for slide 4, click **Format** on the menu bar, click **Slide Color Scheme**, then click the **Custom tab**

   The eight colors for the selected color scheme appear.

8. In the Scheme colors section, click the **Accent and hyperlink color box**, then click **Change Color**

   The Accent and Hyperlink Color dialog box opens.

9. Click the **Standard tab**, click the **plum color cell** in the fifth row from the bottom on the far right, as shown in Figure C-22

   The Current color and the New color appear in the box in the lower-right of the dialog box.

10. Click **OK**, click **Add As Standard Scheme**, then click **Apply to All**

    PowerPoint updates the color scheme on all your slides, and the ribbons change to plum. The next time you open the Color Scheme dialog box in this presentation, your new scheme will appear, along with the existing schemes.

FIGURE C-20: Color Scheme dialog box

Current color scheme has black border

Choose this color scheme

FIGURE C-21: Gradient tab of Fill Effects dialog box

Step 5

Shading styles section

Shading variants of selected shading style

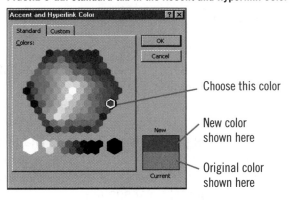

FIGURE C-22: Standard tab in the Accent and Hyperlink Color dialog box

Choose this color

New color shown here

Original color shown here

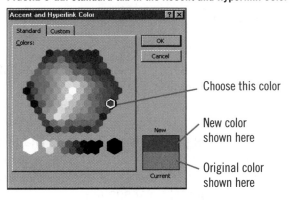

TABLE C-1: Color scheme elements

scheme element	description
Background color	Color of the slide's canvas, or background
Text and lines color	Used for text and drawn lines; contrasts with the background color
Shadows color	Color of the shadow of the text or other object; generally a darker shade of the background color
Title text color	Used for slide title; like the text and line colors, contrasts with the background color
Fills color	Contrasts with both the background and the text and line colors
Accent color	Colors used for other objects on slides, such as bullets
Accent and hyperlink colors	Colors used for accent objects and for hyperlinks you insert
Accent and followed hyperlink color	Color used for accent objects and for hyperlinks after they have been clicked

Correcting Text Automatically

As you enter text into your presentation, the AutoCorrect feature in PowerPoint automatically replaces misspelled words and corrects some capitalization mistakes, whether on slides or in speaker notes, without bringing up a dialog box or a menu. For example, if you type "THursday" instead of "Thursday," PowerPoint corrects it as soon as you type it. If there is a word you often type incorrectly, for example, if you type "tehm" instead of "them," you can create an AutoCorrect entry that corrects that misspelled word whenever you type it in a presentation. After reviewing the presentation, Maria uses the AutoCorrect feature as she adds one more slide, thanking the employees for their support.

1. Click the **slide icon** ☐ for slide 5 in the Outline pane, hold down **[Shift]**, then click the **New Slide button** 🖼 on the Standard toolbar
   A new slide 6 with the bulleted list AutoLayout appears.

2. Click **Tools** on the menu bar, then click **AutoCorrect**
   The AutoCorrect dialog box opens, as shown in Figure C-23. The top part of the dialog box contains check boxes that have PowerPoint automatically change two capital letters at the beginning of a word to a single capital letter, capitalize the first letter of a sentence and the names of days, and correct capitalization errors caused by accidental use of the Caps Lock key. The fifth check box, Replace text as you type, tells PowerPoint to change any of the mistyped words listed on the left in the scroll box in the lower part of the dialog box with the correct word listed on the right. The scroll box contains customized entries. For example, if you type (c), PowerPoint will automatically change it to ©, the copyright symbol. See Table C-2 for a summary of AutoCorrect options.

3. Click any check boxes that are not selected

4. In the Replace text as you type section, click the **down scroll arrow** to view all the current text replacement entries, noticing that there is already an entry to automatically replace cafe with café, then click **OK**
   To test the AutoCorrect feature, you decide to enter incorrect text on the sixth slide. As you type text in the following step, watch what happens to that word when you press [Spacebar].

5. Click the **title placeholder**, then type **THank You**
   As soon as you pressed [Spacebar] after typing the word "THank," PowerPoint automatically corrected it to read "Thank." You'll make another intentional error in the next step.

6. Click the **main text placeholder**, type **Sales reps adn managers**, then press **[Enter]**
   As soon as you pressed [Spacebar] after typing the word "adn," PowerPoint automatically corrected it to read "and."

7. Type **CDVision(tm) advisors**, then click outside the main text object
   As soon as you typed the closing parenthesis, PowerPoint automatically changed the (tm) to the trademark symbol ™.

8. Click the **Slide Sorter View button** 🔲, then compare your screen to Figure C-24

9. Click **View** on the menu bar, click **Header and Footer**, click the **Notes and Handouts tab**, click in the **Footer text box**, type your name, then click **Apply to All**
   Now your name appears in the slide footer when you print the presentation, making it easier to find your printout if you are sharing the printer.

10. Save your presentation, print the slides as handouts, six slides to a page, then exit PowerPoint

QuickTip

In order for most automatic corrections to take effect, you must first press [Spacebar], [Enter], or [Tab] after the word. The exceptions are the three symbols that end in parentheses, which take effect immediately.

FIGURE C-23: AutoCorrect dialog box

Automatic correction options

Type your own custom AutoCorrect entries here

Default AutoCorrect entries

FIGURE C-24: The final presentation

New slide with corrected text

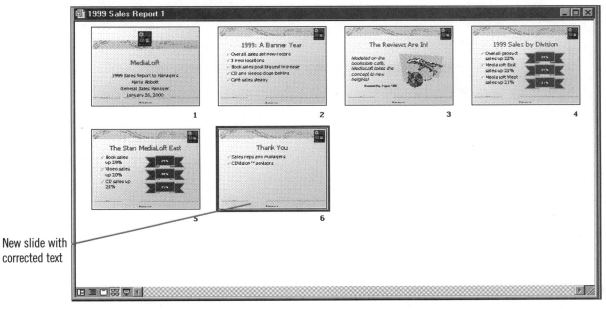

TABLE C-2: AutoCorrect options

option	action
Turn off AutoCorrect	Click to remove all the check marks in the AutoCorrect dialog box
Edit an AutoCorrect entry	Select the entry in the list, click in the With text box, correct the entry, and click Replace
Delete an AutoCorrect entry	Highlight the entry in the scroll box and click Delete
Rename an AutoCorrect entry	Select the entry in the list, click in the Replace text box, click Delete, type a new name in the Replace box, and click Add

PowerPoint 2000

Practice

▶ Concepts Review

Label the elements of the PowerPoint window shown in Figure C-25.

FIGURE C-25

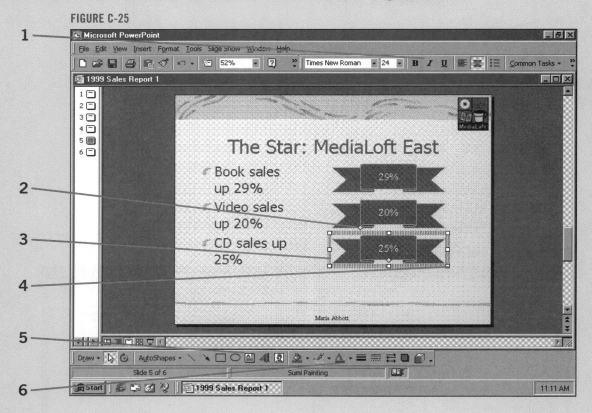

Match each term or button with the statement that describes it.

7. Word-processing box   c
8. Text label   — d
9. 🖻   — b
10. 🄰 ▾   —. a
11. Sizing handles — e

- **a.** Button that changes the text color
- **b.** Creates a text object on a slide
- **c.** Small boxes that surround an object when it is selected
- **d.** A text object that does not word wrap
- **e.** A text object made by dragging to create a box after clicking the Text Box button

Select the best answer from the list of choices.

12. How do you change the size of a PowerPoint object?
- **a.** Drag a sizing handle
- **b.** Click the Resize button
- **c.** Drag the adjustment handle
- **d.** You can't change the size of a PowerPoint object

13. What would you use to position objects at a specific place on a slide?
- **a.** PowerPoint placeholders
- **b.** PowerPoint guides and rulers
- **c.** PowerPoint grid lines
- **d.** PowerPoint anchor lines

Skills Review

1. **Open an existing presentation.**
   a. Open the file PPT C-2 from your Project Disk.
   b. Save it as "Cafe Report."
2. **Draw and modify an object.**
   a. On slide 3, add the AutoShape Lightning Bolt from the Basic Shapes category on the AutoShapes menu. Make it as large as possible from the upper-left corner of the slide. It should partially cover the text.
   b. On the Line Color pop-up menu, click No Line.
   c. Change the fill color to the dark pink color named Follow Accent and Hyperlink Scheme Color.
   d. Click the Shadow button on the Drawing toolbar, then click the Shadow Style 2 button.
   e. Use the appropriate Flip command from the Draw menu on the Drawing toolbar to change the direction of the bolt so it points from the upper-right to the lower-left.
   f. Send the object to the back, then deselect the object and save the document.
3. **Edit drawing objects.**
   a. On slide 6, resize the arrow object so it is about ½" shorter.
   b. Make two copies of the arrow and arrange them to the right of the first one so that they are pointing in succession to the purple box.
   c. Insert the text "Products" on the left arrow object, "Satisfaction" on the middle arrow, and on the right arrow, insert "Growth." Enlarge the arrows so that all the text fits and then reposition them as necessary.
4. **Align and group objects.**
   a. On slide 6, place a text box on the cube, enter "Success" in it, center the text box on the cube, then group the text box and the cube.
   b. Select the four graphics on slide 6 and align their middles.
   c. Change the objects' text font to Arial italic. Enlarge the cube as necessary so the word "Success" fits in it.
   d. Select only the three arrow objects, click the Draw menu button on the Drawing toolbar, then point to Align or Distribute, and click Distribute Horizontally.
   e. Group the three arrow objects and the cube.
   f. Display the guides, then move the vertical guide left to about 4.17, and the horizontal guide down to about 2.50.
   g. Align the grouped object so its bottom-left resize handle snaps to where the guides intersect. If your object does not snap to the guides, click the Draw menu button, point to Snap, and make sure the To Grid command on the Snap menu is selected (it should look indented).
   h. Right-click in an empty area of the slide, then hide the guides.
5. **Add and arrange text.**
   a. Add a fourth item to slide 2 that reads "Next steps."
   b. Near the bottom of the slide, below the graphic, create a word-processing box about 3" wide, and in it enter the text "A relaxing café is a reading haven."
   c. Drag the word "relaxing" in front of the word "reading."
   d. Open the presentation PPT C-3 in Slide Sorter view and copy slide 3 ("The Reviews Are In!") to the Clipboard, then close the PPT C-3 presentation. In the Cafe Report presentation, switch to Slide Sorter view, then paste the copied slide after slide 5.
   e. Use the Slides from Files command on the Insert menu to insert slide 2 ("1999: A Banner Year") from the PPT C-3 presentation after slide 6 ("The Reviews Are In!") in the Cafe Report presentation.
   f. Switch to Outline view, import the Word file PPT C-4 to the end of the presentation. Check each slide's formatting. (*Hint:* If the program tells you that you needto install this feature, insert your Office 2000 CD and click OK.).

6. Format text.

    a. Go to slide 2 in Slide view and select the entire word-processing box so that formatting commands will apply to all the text in the box.

    b. Change the font color to the purple color in the current color scheme, then increase its size once.

    c. Select the entire main text object.

    d. Click the Bullets button on the Formatting toolbar to add bullets to the list.

    e. Go to slide 8, drag to select all the text on the cube, then change the text color to light blue.

    f. Go to slide 2, select the entire main text object, then click the Center alignment button.

    g. Use the Replace command on the Edit menu to replace all occurrences of "sellers" with "performers." Make sure you capitalize the second occurrence.

    h. On slide 2, replace the font of the main text object and the word-processing box with Arial.

    i. Use the Replace Fonts command on the Format menu to change all instances of the Times New Roman font in the presentation to Arial.

    j. Go to slide 1 and change the title text font to Arial Black, 48 points.

    k. Deselect the text object, then save your changes.

7. Customize the color scheme and background.

    a. Open the Color Scheme dialog box.

    b. Click the upper-left color scheme then apply it to all the slides.

    c. Open the Background dialog box, then the Fill Effects dialog box.

    d. On the Gradient tab, select a two-color gradient, picking the light brown that represents Follow Accent and Followed Hyperlink Scheme color as the first color, and the off-white that represents the Follow Background Scheme color as the second color. Select the Diagonal up option and the first variant. Apply this background to all slides.

    e. Open the Color Scheme dialog box.

    f. On the Custom tab, change the color of the Title text on all slides to a brighter shade of purple.

    g. Add the new scheme as a Standard Scheme, and check that it is available on the Standard tab.

    h. Add the Canvas texture to the background of slide 1.

8. Correct text automatically.

    a. Go to slide 5 and turn on Caps Lock.

    b. After the third bullet, add a fourth bullet that reads "Herbal teas." Notice how PowerPoint reverses the capitalization as soon as you press [Spacebar].

    c. For the next bullet, enter the text "Give additional suggestions by thursday." and press [Spacebar]. Notice that PowerPoint automatically capitalizes the word "Thursday" for you.

    d. Check the spelling in the presentation and make any necessary changes.

    e. Go to slide 1, view the final slide show, and evaluate your presentation.

    f. Add your name to the footer of all notes and handouts.

    g. Save your changes, print the slides as handouts, six slides per page, and then close the presentation and exit PowerPoint.

▶ Independent Challenges

1. In this unit, you learned that when you work with multiple objects on a PowerPoint slide, there are three ways to arrange them so your information appears neat and well organized. Write a one-page summary explaining how to perform each of these tasks in PowerPoint:

    a. Lining up objects so that their tops, bottoms, sides or middles are in a straight line.

    b. Combining multiple objects into one object, and why you would want to do this.

    c. Adjusting objects so that one is in front of or in back of another.

2. You work for Chicago Language Systems (CLS), a major producer of language teaching CD-ROMs with accompanying instructional books. Twice a year, the company holds title meetings to determine the new title list for the following production term and to decide which current CD titles need to be revised. As the director of acquisitions, you chair the September Title Meeting and present the basic material for discussion.

To complete this independent challenge:

a. Open the file PPT C-5 on your Project Disk and save it as "Title Meeting 9-26-00".

b. Add an appropriate design template to the presentation.

c. Insert the Word Outline PPT C-6 from your Project Disk after slide 6. Examine each of the three new slides and apply Italic formatting to all product and Book titles.

d. Format the text so that the most important information is the most prominent.

e. Add appropriate shapes that amplify the most important parts of the slide content. Format the objects using color and shading. Use the Align, Group, and stacking commands to organize your shapes.

f. Evaluate the color scheme and the background colors. Make any changes you feel will enhance the presentation.

g. Spell check, view the final slide show, and evaluate your presentation. Make any necessary changes.

h. Add your name as footer text on the handouts, save the presentation and print the slides as handouts.

3. The Software Learning Company is dedicated to the design and development of instructional software that helps college students learn software applications. You need to design five new logos for the company that incorporate the new company slogan: "Software is a snap!" The marketing group will decide which of the five designs looks best. Create your own presentation slides, but assume that the company colors are blue and green.

To complete this independent challenge:

a. Sketch your logos and slogan designs on a piece of paper. What text and graphics do you need for the slides?

b. Create a new blank presentation, and save it as "Software Learning" to your Project Disk.

c. Create five different company logos, each one on a separate slide. Use the shapes on the AutoShapes menu, and enter the company slogan, using the Text tool. (*Hint*: Use the Title only AutoLayout.) The logo and the marketing slogan should match each other in tone, size, and color; and the logo objects should be grouped together to make it easier for other employees to copy and paste. Use shadings and shadows appropriately.

d. Add a background color if it is appropriate for your logo design.

e. Spell check, view the final slide show, and evaluate your presentation. Make any necessary changes.

f. Add your name as footer text, save the presentation, and print the slides and notes pages (if any).

4. MediaLoft management is planning to offer 401(k) retirement plans to its employees. The Human Resources Department has asked you to construct a presentation containing general information about 401(k) plans for all MediaLoft employees.

To complete this independent challenge:

a. Connect to the Internet, use your browser to go to http://www.course.com/illustrated/ medialoft, and click the Human Resources link. Click the Employee Benefits: 401(k) Plans link, and read the information listed there.

b. Use the information you learn from the MediaLoft site to construct a presentation about 401(k) plans that MediaLoft's employees will find useful and interesting. On the title slide, title the presentation "401(k) Plans: What Employees Need to Know". The presentation should contain at least five slides, including the title slide. It should explain what 401(k) plans are, why someone should have one, and what their advantages are. Disconnect from the Internet when you are done.

c. Save the presentation as "401(k) Plans" to your Project Disk.

d. Apply a template to the presentation, customize the slide background, create a new color scheme, and save the color scheme as a standard scheme.

e. Use text formatting as necessary to make text visible and help emphasize important points.

f. At least one slide should contain two or more drawing objects with text in them. Customize their size and color.

g. Add your name as a footer to the slides and handouts, spell check the presentation, view the final presentation, save the final version, then print the slides and handouts.

► Visual Workshop

Create a one-slide presentation that looks like the one shown in Figures C-26. Use a text box for each bullet. Add your name as a footer on the slide. Group the objects in each logo. Save the presentation as "Bowman Logos" to your Project Disk, then print the slide in Slide view. (*Hint:* The top design uses the 3-D menu.) If you don't have the exact fonts, use something similar.

FIGURE C-26

Enhancing
a Presentation

Objectives

- ▶ **Insert clip art**
- ▶ **Insert, crop, and scale a picture**
- ▶ **Embed a chart**
- ▶ **Enter and edit data in the datasheet**
- ▶ **Format a chart**
- ▶ **Use slide show commands**
- ▶ **Create tables in PowerPoint**
- ▶ **Set slide show timings and transitions**
- ▶ **Set slide animation effects**

After completing the content of your presentation, you can supplement your slide text with clip art or graphics, charts, and other visuals that help communicate your content and keep your slide show visually interesting. In this unit, you learn how to insert three of the most common visual enhancements: a clip art image, a picture, and a chart. These objects are created in other programs. After you add the visuals, you rehearse the slide show and add special effects. ✒ Maria Abbot has changed her presentation based on feedback from her colleagues. Now she wants to revise the sales presentation to make it easier to understand and more interesting to watch.

PowerPoint 2000

Inserting Clip Art

PowerPoint has more than 1000 professionally designed images, called **clip art**, that you can place in your presentation. Using clip art is the easiest and fastest way to enhance your presentations. In Microsoft Office, clip art is stored in a file index system called a **gallery** that sorts the clip art into categories. You can open the Clip Gallery in one of three ways: double-click a clip art placeholder from an AutoLayout; use the Insert Clip Art button 🖼 on the Drawing toolbar; or choose Picture, then Clip Art on the Insert menu. As with drawing objects, you can modify clip art images by changing their shape, size, fill, or shading. Clip art is the most widely used method of enhancing presentations, and it is available from many sources outside the Clip Gallery, including the World Wide Web (WWW) and collections on CD-ROMs. ✎ Maria wants to add a picture from the Clip Gallery to one of the slides and then adjust its size and placement.

Steps 1 2 3 4

1. Start PowerPoint, open the presentation **PPT D-1** from your Project Disk, save it as **1999 Sales Presentation 2**, click **Window** on the menu bar, click **Arrange All**, then click the **slide icon** ⬒ for slide 2 in the outline pane
   The 1999: A Banner Year slide appears.

2. Click **Tools** on the menu bar, click **Customize**, click the **Options tab** in the Customize dialog box, click **Reset my usage data** to restore the default settings, click **Yes** in the alert box or dialog balloon, then click **Close**

3. Click the **Common Tasks menu button** on the Formatting toolbar, then click **Slide Layout**
   The Slide Layout dialog box opens with the Bulleted List AutoLayout selected.

4. Click the **Text & Clip Art AutoLayout** (third row, first column), then click **Apply**
   PowerPoint applies the Text and Clip Art AutoLayout to the slide, which makes the existing text object narrower, automatically reduces its font size from 32 points to 28 points, and inserts a clip art placeholder, where you will place the clip art object.

5. Double-click the **clip art placeholder**
   The Microsoft Clip Gallery dialog box opens with the Pictures tab visible, similar to Figure D-1.

6. Scroll down to and click the **Flags category**
   If the Flags category doesn't appear, select a different category.

7. Position the mouse pointer over the **Mountains graphic** whose ScreenTip says "mountains", click the **graphic**, then on the pop-up menu, click the **Insert Clip icon** 🖼 (the top icon)
   The picture of the mountain with a flag on it appears on the right side of the slide. In addition, the Picture toolbar might open automatically. If you don't have the Mountains picture in your Clip Gallery, select a similar picture. If you use the Insert Clip Art button 🖼 on the Drawing toolbar or the Picture command on the Insert menu to insert a clip art image, the Clip Gallery stays open, which is useful in situations where you want to insert more than one picture at a time.

8. Place the pointer over the **lower-right sizing handle** and drag the handle up and to the left about ½"

9. With the clip art object still selected, hold down **[Shift]**, click the **bulleted list**, click the **Draw menu button** on the Drawing toolbar, point to **Align or Distribute**, click **Align Middle**, then click in a blank area to deselect the objects
   The text object and the clip art object align vertically. Compare your screen to Figure D-2, and make any necessary corrections.

FIGURE D-1: Microsoft Clip Gallery dialog box

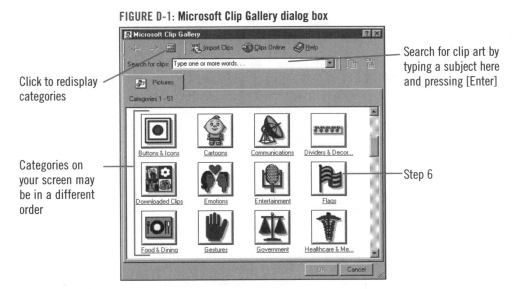

Click to redisplay categories

Search for clip art by typing a subject here and pressing [Enter]

Categories on your screen may be in a different order

Step 6

FIGURE D-2: Slide with graphic resized and repositioned

Text object and graphic are middle aligned

Text object automatically becomes smaller

Find more clips online

If you can't find the clips you need in the Clip Gallery, you can easily use clips from the Clip Gallery Live Web site. To get clips from the Microsoft Clip Gallery Live Web site, click Clips Online in the Insert ClipArt dialog box, then click OK. This will launch your Web browser and automatically connect you to the site. Read carefully and accept the License Agreement, which specifies how you are permitted to use clips from this site. The Clip Gallery Live window opens. You can preview and download (import) clips from four tabs: Clip Art, Pictures (photographs), Sounds, and Motion (animated graphics). You can search the site by keyword or browse by category. Each clip you download is automatically inserted into the Clip Gallery. Figure D-3 shows some of the clip art in the Transportation category.

FIGURE D-3: Microsoft Clip Gallery Live Web site

Inserting, Cropping, and Scaling a Picture

A picture in PowerPoint is a scanned photograph, a piece of line art, clip art, or other artwork that is created in another program and inserted into a PowerPoint presentation. You can insert 20 types of pictures using the Insert Picture command. As with other PowerPoint objects, you can move or crop an inserted picture. **Cropping** a picture means to hide a portion of the picture if you don't want to include all of the original. Although you can easily change a picture's size by dragging a corner resize handle, you can also **scale** it to change its size by a specific percentage. ✏️ Maria inserts a picture that has previously been saved to a file, crops and scales it, and then adjusts its background.

Steps 1 2 3 4

1. Go to **slide 6**, titled "Reasons for Our Growth," click the **Common Tasks menu button** on the Formatting toolbar, click **Slide Layout**, click the **Text & Object AutoLayout** (fourth row, first column), then click **Apply**

2. Double-click the **object placeholder**
   The Insert Object dialog box opens.

3. Click the **Create from file option button** to select it
   The dialog box changes to include a text box that will contain the filename of the object you will insert.

4. Click **Browse**, click the **Look in list arrow**, click the drive containing your Project Disk, click **PPT D-2** in the Look in list, click **OK**, then click **OK** in the Insert Object dialog box
   The picture appears on the slide, and the Picture toolbar automatically opens. See Figure D-4. The slide would have more impact without the sun image.

5. Click the **Crop button** 📐 on the Picture toolbar, then place the cursor over the top, middle sizing handle of the tree picture
   The pointer changes to ┿.

6. Drag the top edge downward until the dotted line indicating the top edge of the picture is below the sun image, as shown in Figure D-5
   As you drag with the cropping tool, the pointer changes to ⊥. But now the picture needs to be larger to fill the space.

7. Click a blank area of the slide to deselect the cropping tool and leave the picture selected

8. Click the **Format Picture button** 🖼️ on the Picture toolbar, click the **Size tab**, under Scale, make sure the **Lock aspect ratio check box** is selected, click and hold the **Height up arrow** until the Height and Width percentages reach **275%**, then click **OK**
   When you are scaling a picture and Lock aspect ratio is checked, the ratio of height to width remains the same. Although you cannot change the colors in this bitmapped (.bmp) object in PowerPoint, you can change its background.

9. With the image still selected, click the **Set Transparent Color button** 🖊️ on the Picture toolbar, then click the **white background** in the image with the pointer 🖊️
   The white background is no longer visible, and the tree contrasts well with the background.

10. Drag the graphic to center it in the blank space, deselect it, then save your changes
    See Figure D-6.

FIGURE D-4: Inserted picture object and Picture toolbar

Picture toolbar may appear in a different position on your screen

Inserted picture object

Crop button

Set Transparent Color button

FIGURE D-5: Using the cropping pointer to crop out the sun image

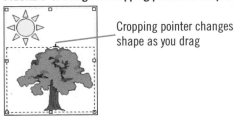

Cropping pointer changes shape as you drag

FIGURE D-6: Completed slide with the cropped and resized graphic

CLUES TO USE

Graphics in PowerPoint

You can insert pictures with a variety of graphics file formats, or file types, in PowerPoint. Most of the clip art that comes with PowerPoint is in **Windows metafile** format and has a **.wmf** file extension. A graphic in .wmf format can be ungrouped into its separate PowerPoint objects and then edited with PowerPoint drawing tools. You can recolor a .wmf graphic by selecting it and clicking the Recolor picture icon on the Picture toolbar, which lets you replace each color in the graphic with another color. You can also recolor any portion of an ungrouped .wmf graphic by selecting it and using the Fill Color drawing tool. If you ungroup a .wmf graphic and find that it has too

many parts, you can regroup them using the Group command on the Draw menu. The clip art you inserted in the last lesson is in .wmf format, and the tree picture you inserted in this lesson is in .bmp format.

You can also save PowerPoint slides as graphics and then use them in other presentations, in graphics programs, and on Web pages. Display the slide you want to save, then click Save As from the File menu. In the Save As dialog box, click the Save as type list arrow, and scroll to the desired graphics format. Name the file, click OK, then click the desired option when the alert box appears asking if you want to save all the slides or only the current slide.

Embedding a Chart

Often, the best way to communicate information is with a visual aid such as a chart. PowerPoint comes with a program called **Microsoft Graph** (often called **Graph**) that you use to create graph charts for your slides. A **graph object** is made up of two components: a **datasheet**, containing the numbers you want to chart, and a **chart**, which is the graphical representation of the datasheet. Table D-1 lists the Graph chart types. When you insert a Graph object into PowerPoint, you are actually embedding it. **Embedding** an object means that the object copy becomes part of the PowerPoint file, but you can double-click on the embedded object to display the tools of the program in which the object was created. You can use these tools to modify the object. If you modify the embedded object, the original object file does not change. ✦ Maria wants to embed a Graph object in the slide containing the 1999 revenue by quarter.

1. Go to **slide 5**, titled "1999 Revenue by Quarter," click the **Common Tasks menu button** on the Formatting toolbar, then click **Slide Layout**
The Slide Layout dialog box opens with the Title only Layout selected.

2. Click the **Chart AutoLayout** (second row, far right), then click **Apply**
The Chart AutoLayout, which contains a chart placeholder, appears on the slide.

Trouble?

If the Graph Formatting toolbar doesn't appear, click View on the menu bar, point to Toolbars, and click the Formatting check box.

3. Double-click the **chart placeholder**
Microsoft Graph opens and embeds a default datasheet and chart into the slide, as shown in Figure D-7. The Graph datasheet consists of rows and columns. The intersection of a row and a column is called a **cell**. Cells are referred to by their row and column location; for example, the cell at the intersection of column A and row 1 is called cell A1. Cells along the left column and top row of the datasheet typically contain **data labels** that identify the data in a column or row; for example, "East" and "1st Qtr" are data labels. Cells below and to the right of the data labels contain the data values that are represented in the Graph chart. Each column and row of data in the datasheet is called a **data series**. Each data series has corresponding **data series markers** in the chart, which are graphical representations such as bars, columns, or pie wedges. The PowerPoint Standard and Formatting toolbars have been replaced with the Microsoft Graph Standard and Formatting toolbars, and the menu bar has changed to include Microsoft Graph commands.

QuickTip

When the Data and Chart menus are present, you are working in Graph. Clicking outside the Graph object returns you to PowerPoint.

4. Move the pointer over the datasheet
The pointer changes to ✛. Cell A1 is the **active cell**, which means that it is selected. The active cell has a heavy black border around it.

5. Click cell **B3**, which currently has the value 46.9 in it
Cell B3 is now the active cell.

6. Click a blank area of the Presentation window to exit Graph and deselect the chart object
Compare your slide to Figure D-8.

FIGURE D-7: Datasheet and chart in the PowerPoint window

Graph menu bar

Graph Formatting toolbar

Data labels

Chart

Active cell

Datasheet containing default data

Data marker corresponds to data series

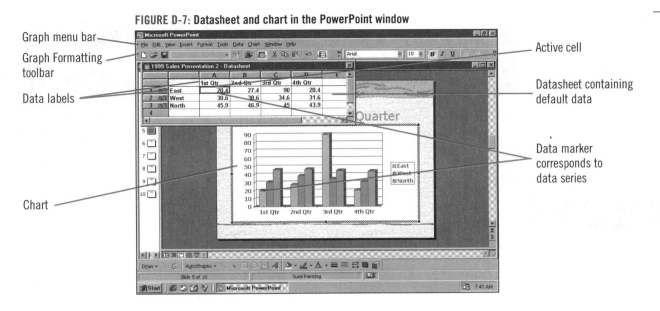

FIGURE D-8: Chart object on a slide

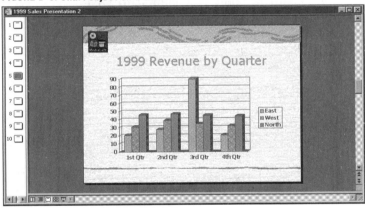

TABLE D-1: Microsoft Graph chart types

chart type	looks like	use to
Column		Track values over time or across categories
Bar		Compare values in categories or over time
Line		Track values over time
Pie		Compare individual values to the whole
XY (Scatter)		Compare pairs of values
Area		Show contribution of each data series to the total over time
Doughnut		Compare individual values to the whole with multiple series
Radar		Show changes in values in relation to a center point
Surface		Show value trends across two dimensions
Bubble		Indicate relative size of data points
Stock		Show stock market information or scientific data
Cylinder, cone, pyramid		Track values over time or across categories

PowerPoint 2000

Entering and Editing Data in the Datasheet

After you embed the default datasheet and chart into your presentation, you need to change the data label and cell information in the sample datasheet to create the chart you need. Although you can import information from a spreadsheet, it is often easier to use Graph and type in the information. As you enter data or make changes to the datasheet, the chart automatically changes to reflect your alterations. ◀ Maria enters the 1999 quarterly sales figures by division that she wants to show to the employees. She first changes the data labels and then the series information in the cells.

Steps 1 2 3 4

1. **Double-click the chart on slide 5**

   The graph is selected and the datasheet appears. The labels representing the quarters across the top are correct, but the row labels need adjusting, and the data needs to be replaced with MediaLoft's quarterly sales figures for each division.

2. **Click the East row label, type MediaLoft East, then press [Enter]**

   After you press [Enter], the first data label changes from East to MediaLoft East (although you cannot see all of it right now), and the data label in row 2, the cell directly below the active cell, becomes selected. Don't worry that the column is not wide enough to accommodate the label; you'll fix that after you enter all the labels.

3. **Type MediaLoft West, press [Tab], then press [↑]**

   Pressing [Tab] moves the active cell one column to the right and pressing [↑] moves it up one row—cell A1 is the active cell. Notice that in the chart itself, below the datasheet, the data labels you typed are now in the legend to the right of the chart.

4. **Position the pointer on top of the column divider to the left of the letter A so that ✛ changes to ↔ and double-click**

   The data label column automatically widens to accommodate all the column label text.

5. **With cell A1 selected, type 600,000, press [Enter], type 300,000, press [Tab], then press [↑] to move to cell B1, to the top of the second data series column**

   Notice that the heights of the columns in the chart change to reflect the numbers you typed.

6. **Enter the rest of the numbers shown in Figure D-9 to complete the datasheet**

Trouble?

The datasheet window can be manipulated in the same ways other windows are. If you can't see a column or a row, use the scroll bars to move another part of the datasheet into view, or resize the datasheet window so you can see all the data.

7. **Click the row 3 row number, then press [Delete]**

   The chart columns adjust to reflect the new information, and the default information in row 3 no longer appears. The chart currently shows the columns grouped by quarter (the legend represents the rows in the datasheet). It would be more effective if the columns were grouped by division (with the legend representing the columns in the datasheet).

8. **Click Data on the menu bar, then click Series in Columns**

   The division labels are now on the horizontal axis, and the quarters are listed in the legend. The groups of data markers (the columns) now represent the sales for each division by quarter. Notice that the small column chart graphics that used to be in the row labels have now moved to the column labels, indicating that the series are now in columns.

9. **Click in the Presentation window outside the chart area, compare your chart to Figure D-10, then save the presentation**

   The datasheet closes, allowing you to see your entire chart. This chart layout clearly shows MediaLoft East's sales have exceeded MediaLoft West's, but that MediaLoft West's sales are increasing steadily.

FIGURE D-9: Datasheet showing MediaLoft's revenue for each quarter

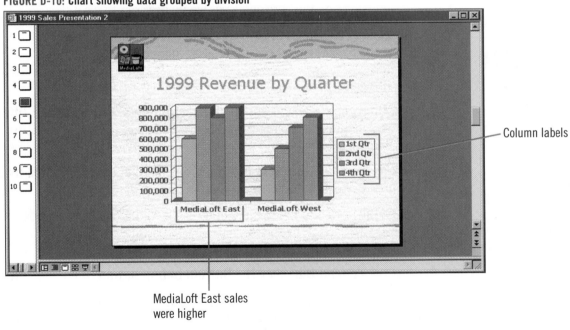

Graphic shows that series are currently in rows

Step 7

Bars automatically show the new values

FIGURE D-10: Chart showing data grouped by division

1999 Revenue by Quarter

Column labels

MediaLoft East sales were higher

Series in Rows vs. Series in Columns

If you have difficulty visualizing the difference between the Series in Rows and the Series in Columns commands on the Data menu, think about the legend. **Series in rows** means that the information in the rows will become the legend in the chart (and the column labels will be on the horizontal axis). **Series in** **Columns** means that the information in the columns will become the legend in the chart (and the row labels will be on the horizontal axis). Microsoft Graph places a small graphic representing the chart type on the axis items that are currently represented by the chart series items (bars, etc.).

PowerPoint 2000

Formatting a Chart

Graph lets you change the appearance of the chart to emphasize certain aspects of the information you are presenting. You can change the chart type, create titles, format the chart labels, move the legend, or add arrows. ✏️ Maria wants to improve the appearance of her chart by formatting the vertical and horizontal axes and by inserting a title.

1. **Double-click** the **chart** to reopen Microsoft Graph, then click the **Close button** in the Datasheet window to close the datasheet
   The Microsoft Graph menu and toolbar remain at the top of the window.

2. Click the **sales numbers** on the vertical axis to select the axis, then click **the Currency Style button** 💲 on the Chart Formatting toolbar
   The numbers on the vertical axis appear with dollar signs and two decimal places. You don't need to show the two decimal places, because all the values are whole numbers.

3. Click the **Decrease Decimal button** ⬚ on the Chart Formatting toolbar twice
   The numbers on the vertical axis now have dollar signs and show only whole numbers. The division names on the horizontal axis would be easier to see if they were larger.

4. Click either of the **division names** on the horizontal axis, click the **Font Size list arrow** on the Chart Formatting toolbar, then click **20**
   The font size changes from 18 points to 20 points for both labels on the horizontal axis. Viewers would understand the chart more readily if it had a title and axis labels.

5. Click **Chart** on the menu bar, click **Chart Options**, then click the **Titles tab**
   The Chart Options dialog box opens, in which you can change the chart title, axes, gridlines, legend, data labels, and the table.

6. Click in the **Chart title text box**, then type **MediaLoft 1999 Sales by Division**
   The preview box changes to show you the chart with the title.

7. Press **[Tab]** twice to move the cursor to the Value (Z) axis text box, then type **Sales**
   In a 3-D chart, the vertical axis is called the Z-axis, and the depth axis, which you don't usually work with, is the Y-axis. See Figure D-11 for the completed Titles tab.

8. Click the **Legend tab**, click the **Bottom option button**, then click **OK**

9. Double-click the border of the **"Sales" label** on the vertical axis, click the **Alignment tab**, drag the **red diamond** in the Orientation section up to a vertical position so the spin box reads 90 degrees, click **OK**, then click a blank area of the Presentation window
   Graph closes and the PowerPoint toolbars and menu bar appear. See Figure D-12.

Customizing Charts

You can easily customize the look of any chart in Microsoft Graph. Click the chart to select it, then double-click any data series element (a column, for example) to open the Format Data Series dialog box. Use the tabs to change the element's fill color, border, shape, or data label. You can even use the same fill effects you apply to a presentation background. In 3-D charts, you can change the chart depth as well as the distances between series.

FIGURE D-11: Titles tab in the Chart Options dialog box

FIGURE D-12: Slide showing formatted chart

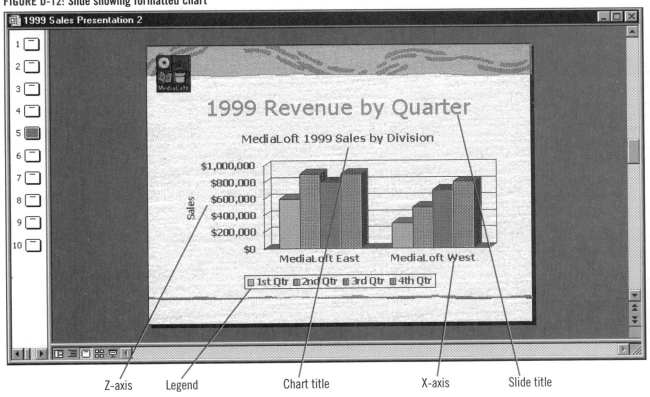

Z-axis   Legend   Chart title   X-axis   Slide title

Using Slide Show Commands

With PowerPoint, you can show a presentation on any compatible computer using Slide Show view. As you've seen, Slide Show view fills your computer screen with the slides of your presentation, showing them one at a time—similar to how a slide projector shows slides. Once your presentation is in Slide Show view, you can use a number of slide show options to tailor the show. For example, you can draw on, or **annotate**, slides or jump to a specific slide. Maria runs a slide show of her presentation and practices using some of the custom slide show options to make her presentation more effective.

1. Go to **slide 1**, then click the **Slide Show button** 🖵
   The first slide of the presentation fills the screen.

2. Press **[Spacebar]**
   Slide 2 appears on the screen. Pressing [Spacebar] or clicking the left mouse button is the easiest way to move through a slide show. You can also use the keys listed in Table D-2. You can also use the Slide Show pop-up menu for on-screen navigation during a slide show.

   QuickTip
   You can also access the Slide Show menu by moving the mouse pointer, then clicking the Slide Show menu icon that appears in the lower-left corner of the screen.

3. Right-click anywhere on the screen, point to **Go** on the pop-up menu, then click **Slide Navigator**
   The Slide Navigator dialog box opens and displays a list of the presentation slides.

4. Click **6**. **Reasons for Our Growth** in the Slide titles list box, then click **Go To**
   The slide show jumps to slide 6. You can emphasize major points in your presentation by annotating the slide during a slide show using the Pen.

5. Right-click the slide, point to **Pointer Options** on the pop-up menu, then click **Pen**
   The pointer changes to ✎.

6. Press and hold **[Shift]** and drag ✎ to draw a line under each of the bulleted points on the slide
   Holding down [Shift] constrains the Pen tool to straight horizontal or vertical lines. Compare your screen to Figure D-13. While the annotation pen is visible, mouse clicks do not advance the slide show. However, you can still move to the next slide by pressing [Spacebar] or [Enter].

7. Right-click to view the Slide Show pop-up menu, point to **Screen**, click **Erase Pen**, then press **[Ctrl][A]**
   The annotations on slide 6 are erased and the pointer returns to ⩊.

   QuickTip
   If you know the slide number of the slide you want to jump to, type the number, then press [Enter].

8. Right-click anywhere on the screen to view the Slide Show pop-up menu, point to **Go**, point to **By Title**, then click **4 1999 Sales by Division** on the pop-up menu
   Slide 4 appears.

9. Press **[Home]**, then click the mouse, press **[Spacebar]**, or press **[Enter]** to advance through the slide show
   After the black slide that indicates the end of the slide show appears, the next click ends the slide show and returns you to Slide view.

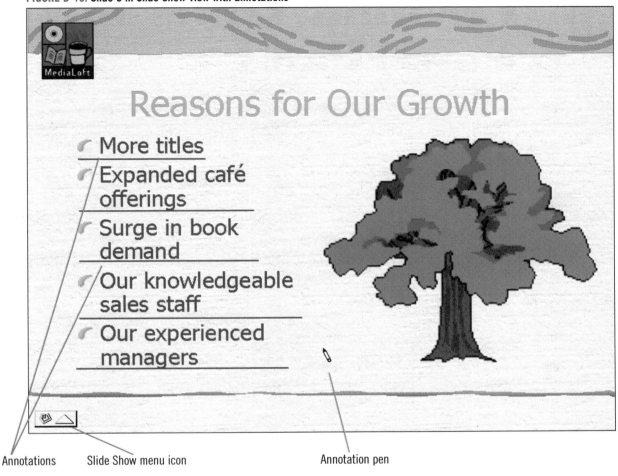

FIGURE D-13: Slide 6 in Slide Show view with annotations

Annotations   Slide Show menu icon   Annotation pen

TABLE D-2: Slide show keyboard controls

control	description
[E]	Erases the annotation drawing
[Enter], [Spacebar], [PgDn], [N], [↓] or [→]	Advances to the next slide
[H]	Displays a hidden slide
[↑] or [PgUp]	Returns to the previous slide
[W]	Changes the screen to white; press again to return
[S]	Pauses the slide show; press again to continue
[B]	Changes the screen to black; press again to return
[Ctrl][P]	Changes pointer to ✎
[CTRL][A]	Changes pointer to ⬚
[Esc]	Stops the slide show

Creating Tables in PowerPoint

As you create your PowerPoint presentations, you may need to insert information in a row and column format. A table you create in PowerPoint is ideal for this type of information layout. There are two ways to create a table in PowerPoint: the Table command on the Insert menu and the Table slide layout. Once you have created a table, you can use the buttons on the Tables and Borders toolbar to format it, as well as the buttons on the Formatting toolbar. Maria uses the Table command on the Insert menu to create a table describing MediaLoft's competition.

Steps

1. **Go to slide 7, click Insert on the menu bar, then click Table**
   The Insert Table dialog box opens, allowing you to specify the number of columns and rows you want in your table. The default of 2 columns is correct but you want 4 rows.

2. **Press [Tab], type 4, then click OK**
   A table with 2 columns and 4 rows appears on the slide, and the Tables and Borders toolbar opens. See Table D-3 to learn about the buttons on this toolbar.

   Trouble?

   If the Tables and Borders toolbar does not open, click View on the menu bar, click Toolbars, then click Tables and Borders. If the toolbar obscures part of the table, drag it out of the way.

3. **Type Seller, press [Tab], type # of Titles, then press [Tab]**

4. **Enter the rest of the table information shown in Figure D-14, pressing [Tab] after each entry except the last one**

5. **Drag the table by its border down below the slide title**
   See Figure D-14. The table would look better if it were formatted.

6. **Drag to select the column headings in the top row of the table**
   The column headings row becomes highlighted.

   QuickTip

   You can change the height or width of any table cell by dragging its top or side borders.

7. **Click the Center Vertically button ▤ on the Tables and Borders toolbar, click the Fill Color list arrow ⬛▾ on the Tables and Borders toolbar, then click the light purple color in the second row**

8. **With the column headings still selected, click the Center button ▤ on the Formatting toolbar, then click in a blank area of the presentation window**
   The column headings are centered horizontally and vertically and the row is filled with purple.

9. **Vertically center the text in the other three rows, then fill these three rows with the light orange color in the second row**
   The table would look better if the last three rows were a little farther away from the cell edges.

   QuickTip

   You can use the Format Table dialog box to apply a diagonal line through any table cell. Click the Borders tab, then click the diagonal line button.

10. **With the bottom three rows still selected, click Format on the menu bar, click Table, click the Text Box tab, click the Left up scroll arrow twice so it reads .2, click OK, click outside the table, then save the presentation**
    The Tables and Borders toolbar closes and the table is no longer selected. Compare your screen with Figure D-15.

FIGURE D-14: The new table before formatting

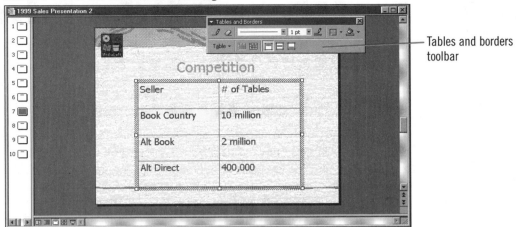

Tables and borders toolbar

FIGURE D-15: The formatted table

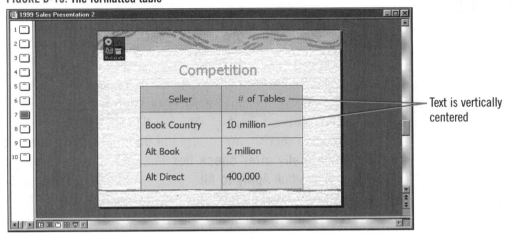

Text is vertically centered

TABLE D-3: The buttons on the Tables and Borders toolbar

button	name	What it does
	Draw Table	Changes the pointer to ✏, which lets you drag to create a table or draw lines in an existing table
	Eraser	Changes the pointer to ⌫, which lets you click any line in a drawn table to erase the line
	Border Style	Lets you change the border style of the next line you draw with the Pencil pointer
1 pt	**Border Width**	Lets you change the width of the next line you draw with the Pencil pointer
	Border Color	Changes the color of any table border
	Outside Border	Lets you choose a border, horizontal, or vertical line for any selected table cell(s)
	Fill Color	Lets you change the fill color of any selected table cell(s)
Table ▾	**Table Menu**	Lets you insert a table, insert or delete rows or columns, merge or split cells, select parts of a table, or modify borders and fills
	Merge Cells	Lets you merge two selected table cells into one
	Split Cells	Lets you split a selected table cell into two cells
	Align top, center vertically, align bottom	Let you change the vertical alignment of selected cell text

Setting Slide Show Timings and Transitions

In a slide show, you can preset when and how each slide appears on the screen. You can set the **slide timing**, which is the amount of time a slide is visible on the screen. Each slide can have the same or different timing. Setting the right slide timing is important because it determines the amount of time you have to discuss the material on each slide. You can also set slide transitions, the special visual and audio effects you apply to a slide that determine how it moves in and out of view during the slide show. Maria decides to set her slide timings for 10 seconds per slide and to set the transitions for all slides but the last one to fade to black before the next slide appears.

1. Click the **Slide Sorter View button** 🔳
   Slide Sorter view shows a miniature image of the slides in your presentation. The number of slides you see on your screen depends on the current zoom setting. Notice that the Slide Sorter toolbar appears below the Standard and Formatting toolbars.

QuickTip

You also can click Slide Show on the menu bar, then click Slide Transition.

2. Right-click one of the slides, then click **Slide Transition** on the pop-up menu
   The Slide Transition dialog box, shown in Figure D-16, opens.

3. In the Advance section, make sure the **On mouse click check box** is selected, click the **Automatically after check box** to select it, type **10** in the Automatically after text box, then click **Apply to All**
   The timing between slides is 10 seconds, which appears under each slide. When you run the slide show, each slide will remain on the screen for 10 seconds. If you finish talking in less time and want to advance more quickly, press [Spacebar] or click the mouse button.

4. Right-click one of the slides, click **Slide Transition** on the pop-up menu, then click the **Effect list arrow** in the top section
   A drop-down menu appears, showing all the transition effects.

QuickTip

You also can click Edit on the menu bar, click Select All, then click the Transition list arrow on the Slide Sorter toolbar to apply a transition effect to all the slides.

5. Scroll down the list, click **Fade Through Black**, note that the Preview picture in the Effect section demonstrates the selected effect, click **Apply to All**, then click in a blank area of the Presentation window to deselect the slide
   As shown in Figure D-17, each slide in Slide Sorter view now has a small transition icon under it, indicating there is a transition effect set for the slides.

6. Click the **transition icon** under any slide
   The previous slide appears briefly, then the transition effect appears; in this case the image fades then the current slide appears.

7. Scroll down the Presentation window, right-click the **last slide**, click **Slide Transition** on the pop-up menu, click the **Effect list arrow**, then click **Split Vertical Out**
   As the preview shows, the last slide will now appear with a split from the center of the screen.

8. Click the **Sound list arrow**, scroll down the list, click **Drum Roll** or choose another sound effect, then click **Apply**
   Make sure you did not click Apply to All this time. The last slide now has a different visual effect and a drum roll transition applied to it.

9. Press [**Home**], click the **Slide Show button** 🖵 and watch the slide show advance
   To move more quickly, press [Spacebar] or [Enter].

10. When you see the black slide at the end of the slide show, press [**Enter**]
    The slide show ends.

FIGURE D-16: Slide Transition dialog box

Click to apply to all slides in the presentation

Click to apply only to selected slide

Click to set transition effect

Set timing characteristics here

FIGURE D-17: Slide Sorter view showing transition effects and timing

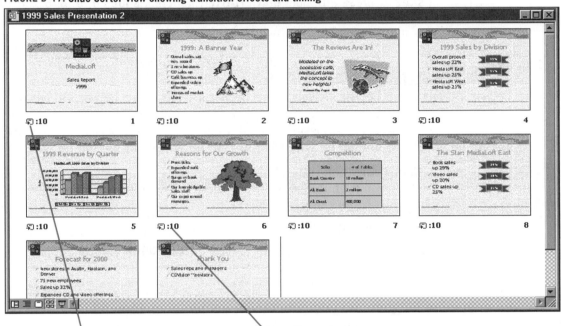

Indicates a slide show transition is set for this slide

Indicates slide will remain on screen for 10 seconds

Rehearsing slide show timing

You can set different slide timings for each slide. For example, you can have the title slide appear for 20 seconds, the second slide for 3 minutes, and so on. You also can set timings by clicking the Rehearse Timings button on the Slide Sorter toolbar or by choosing the Rehearse Timings command on the Slide Show menu. The Rehearsal dialog box shown in Figure D-18 opens. It contains buttons to pause between slides and to advance to the next slide. After opening the Rehearsal dialog box, practice giving your presentation. PowerPoint keeps track of how long each slide appears and sets the timing accordingly. You can view your rehearsed timings in Slide Sorter view. The next time you run the slide show, you can use the timings you rehearsed.

FIGURE D-18: Rehearsal dialog box

Click to pause

Time elapsed while viewing this slide

Click to repeat and set clock to zero again for this slide

Total elapsed time

Setting Slide Animation Effects

Animation effects let you control how the graphics and main points in your presentation appear on the screen during a slide show. You can animate text, images, or even individual chart elements, or you can add sound effects. Keep in mind that the animation effects you choose give a certain "flavor" to your presentation. They can be serious and businesslike or humorous. Choose appropriate effects for your presentation content and audience. ✐ Maria wants to animate the text and graphics of several slides in her presentation.

Steps

1. Click **slide 2**, press and hold down **[Ctrl]**, then click **slides 4**, **6**, **8**, **9**, and **10**
   The selected slides have bullets on them. The bullets can be animated to appear on the slide individually when you click the mouse during the slide show.

2. On the Slide Sorter toolbar, click the **Preset Animation list arrow**, then click **Fly From Left**
   Slide 10 previews the bullets flying in from the left side of the slide, and because this slide has a custom animation applied to it, you also hear the drum roll. When you run the slide show, instead of appearing all at once, the bullets of the selected slides will appear one at a time, "flying" in from the left each time you click the mouse button.

3. Click **slide 1**, then run the slide show
   The bullets fly in from the left. (Some of the graphics on these slides may also fly in from the left.) To set custom animation effects, the target slide must be in Slide view.

4. Double-click **slide 6** to view it in the previous view, which in this case is Slide view, click **Slide Show** on the menu bar, then click **Custom Animation**
   The Custom Animation dialog box opens. Objects that are already animated appear in the Animation Order section in the order in which they will be animated.

5. In the Check to animate slide objects list box, click **Object 3**
   Make sure you do not click the Object 3 check box and remove its checkmark. Object 3 represents the tree, which becomes highlighted in the preview. See Figure D-19.

6. Click the **Effects tab**, click the **top left list arrow** in the Entry animation and sound section, click **Dissolve**, click **Preview** in the upper-right corner of the dialog box to see the new animation effect, then click **OK**

7. Change the animation effect to **Dissolve** for the mountain graphic on slide 2 and the airplane graphic on slide 3

8. Run the Slide Show again from slide 1, then return to Slide Sorter view
   The special effects make the presentation easier to understand and more interesting.

9. Click the **Zoom text box** on the Standard toolbar, type **50**, press **[Enter]**, click **Window** on the menu bar, then click **Fit to Page**
   Figure D-20 shows the completed presentation in Slide Sorter view at 50% zoom.

10. Click **View** on the menu bar, click **Header and Footer**, click the **Notes and Handouts** tab, type your name in the Footer text box, click **Apply to All**, save your presentation, print it as handouts, six slides per page, then exit PowerPoint

QuickTip
Use the ScreenTips to see the names of the Slide Sorter toolbar buttons.

QuickTip
If you want a grouped object, like the ribbons on slides 4 and 8, to fly in individually, then you must ungroup them first.

QuickTip
To preview animation in Normal view, Slide Sorter view, or Slide view, click Slide Show on the menu bar, then click Animation Preview.

FIGURE D-19: Custom Animation dialog box

Slide objects listed here with a check mark are added to Animation order list below

Click here to change animation effects

Preview box

Click to preview special effects

FIGURE D-20: Completed presentation in Slide Sorter view

Presentation Checklist

You should always rehearse your slide show. If possible, rehearse your presentation in the room and with the computer that you will use. Use the following checklist to prepare for the slide show.

✔ Is **PowerPoint** or **PowerPoint Viewer** installed on the computer?

✔ Is your **presentation file** on the hard drive of the computer you will be using? Try putting a shortcut for the file on the desktop. Do you have a backup copy of your presentation file on a floppy disk?

✔ Is the **projection device** working correctly? Can the slides be seen from the back of the room?

✔ Do you know how to control **room lighting** so that the audience can both see your slides and their handouts and notes? You may want to designate someone to control the lights if the controls are not close to you.

✔ Will the **computer** be situated so you can advance and annotate the slides yourself? If not, designate someone to advance them for you.

✔ Do you have enough copies of your **handouts**? Bring extras. Decide when to hand them out, or whether you prefer to have them waiting at the audience members' places when they enter.

PowerPoint 2000

ENHANCING A PRESENTATION POWERPOINT D-19 ◄

Practice

▶ Concepts Review

Label each element of the PowerPoint window shown in Figure D-21.

FIGURE D-21

Match each term with the statement that describes it.

8. Chart
9. Embedded object
10. Animation effect
11. Data series markers
12. Clip Gallery
13. Scaling

a. Resizing an object by a specific percentage
b. A graphic representation of a datasheet
c. Graphic representations of data series
d. The way bulleted items and images appear on a slide
e. A copy of an object from which you can access another program's tools
f. A file index system that organizes images

Select the best answer from the list of choices.

14. PowerPoint animation effects let you control
   a. The order in which text and objects are animated.
   b. The direction from which animated objects appear.
   c. Which text and images are animated.
   d. All of the above.

15. Which of the following is *not* true of a Microsoft Graph chart?
   a. A graph is made up of a datasheet and chart.
   b. You can double-click a chart to view its corresponding datasheet.
   c. An active cell has a black selection rectangle around it.
   d. You cannot import data from other programs into a datasheet.

▶ Skills Review

1. Insert clip art.

a. Open the presentation PPT D-3 on your Project Disk, save it as "CD Product Report" to your Project Disk.

b. Go to slide 2 and insert the musical notes graphic from the Music category in the Clip Gallery.

c. On the Size tab of the Format Picture dialog box, deselect Relative to original picture size, scale the graphic to 125% of its current size, and center it in the blank space.

d. Align the top of the main text placeholder with the top of the graphic, and adjust their position as necessary.

2. Insert, crop, and scale a picture.

a. Change the layout of slide 6 to the Text & Object layout, and insert PPT D-4 into the object placeholder.

b. Crop about ¾" off the left side of the picture.

c. Align the tops of the text box and the graphic.

d. Scale the graphic to an appropriate percentage of its original size so it is approximately the same size as the main text box.

e. Reposition the graphic, then make the background of the graphic transparent.

3. Embed a chart.

a. Go to slide 3, "1999 CD Sales by Quarter," and apply the Chart AutoLayout.

b. Start Microsoft Graph.

c. Move the mouse pointer around on the datasheet and note the different pointer shapes.

d. Deselect the chart object.

4. Enter and edit data in the datasheet.

a. Open Graph again, and for the row 1 datasheet label, enter "MediaLoft East."

b. Enter the information shown in Table D-4 into the datasheet and widen the column to fit all the data.

c. Delete any unused rows of default data.

d. Place the Data Series in Columns.

TABLE D-4

	1st Qtr	2nd Qtr	3rd Qtr	4th Qtr
MediaLoft East	36	40	45	43
MediaLoft West	44	50	52	53

5. Format a chart.

a. Close the datasheet but leave Graph running.

b. Change the region names on the X-axis to 20 points.

c. Apply the Currency Style with no decimals to the values on the vertical axis.

d. Insert the chart title "1999 CD Sales."

e. Add the text "Sales in 000s" to the Z-axis, then change the orientation of the Z-axis to vertical.

f. Place the legend below the graphic.

g. Exit Graph.

6. Use slide show commands.

a. Begin the slide show at slide 1, then proceed through the slide show to slide 3.

b. On slide 3, use the Pen to draw straight-line annotations under the labels on the horizontal axis.

c. Erase the pen annotations, then change the pointer back to an arrow.

d. Go to slide 2 using the Go command on the slide show pop-up menu.

e. Use [End] to move to the last slide.

f. Return to Slide view.

7. Create a table.

a. Add a slide using the title only format after slide 2.

b. Add the slide title "CD Sales by Type."

c. Insert a PowerPoint table with 2 columns and 5 rows.

   d. For the header row, enter Type and Sales.

   e. In the left column, add the following types: Rock, Folk, Classical, and Jazz/Blues.

   f. In the right column, add realistic sales figures for each CD type.

   g. Reposition the table so it doesn't obscure the slide title.

   h. Format the table using fills, horizontal and vertical alignment, or any other features.

8. Set slide show timings and transitions.

   a. Switch to Slide Sorter view.

   b. Open the Slide Transition dialog box using the pop-up menu.

   c. Specify that all slides should advance after 15 seconds, unless the mouse is clicked first.

   d. Apply the Box Out transition effect to all slides.

   e. In Slide Sorter view, preview the transition effect on two slides.

   f. Apply the Cover Down transition effect to the last slide in the presentation.

   g. View the slide show to verify the transitions are correct.

9. Set slide animation effects.

   a. In Slide Sorter view, apply the Peek from Right animation effect to the bulleted list on slide 5.

   b. Go to slide 2 in Slide or Normal view, and using the Custom Animation dialog box, apply the Dissolve effect to the Music graphic and preview the effect in the dialog box.

   c. Specify that the bulleted list text object should spiral in after the musical notes graphic appears, and preview the effect. (*Hint:* Check the Order & Timing tab to make sure the musical notes graphic is first in the list.)

   d. Run the slide show from the beginning to check the animation effects.

   e. Save the presentation.

   f. Add your name as a footer to the notes and handouts, then print the presentation as handouts, six slides per page.

   g. Close the presentation and exit PowerPoint.

► Independent Challenges

1. You are a financial management consultant for Pacific Coast Investments, located in San José, California. One of your primary responsibilities is to give financial seminars on different financial investments and how to determine which funds to invest in. In this challenge, you enhance the look of the slides by adding and formatting objects and adding animation effects and transitions.

  To complete this independent challenge:

   a. Open the file PPT D-5 on your Project Disk, and save it as "Fund Seminar" to your Project Disk.

   b. Add your name as the footer on all slides and handouts.

   c. Apply the Chart layout to slide 6, and enter the data in Table D-5 into the datasheet.

   d. Format the chart. Add titles as necessary.

   e. Add an appropriate clip art item to slide 2.

   f. On slide 4, use the Align, Group, and Order commands to organize the shapes.

   g. Spell check the presentation, then save it.

   h. View the slide show, evaluate your presentation and add a template of your choice. Make changes if necessary.

TABLE D-5

	1 year	3 year	5 year	10 year
Bonds	4.2%	5.2%	7.9%	9.4%
Stocks	7.5%	8.3%	10.8%	12.6%
Mutual Funds	6.1%	6.3%	6.4%	6.1%

   i. Set animation effects, slide transitions, and slide timings, keeping in mind that your audience includes potential investors who need the information you are presenting to make decisions about where to put their hard-earned money. View the slide show again.

   j. Print the slides of the presentation as handouts, six slides per page, then close the presentation.

2. You are the communications director at Heridia Design, Inc, an international advertising agency. One of your responsibilities is to create an on-screen presentation for a presentation contest at the National Association of Advertising Agencies (NAAA) convention. Create a presentation using any type of company. The presentation can be aimed to either convince or educate your audience.

To complete this independent challenge:

a. Plan and create the slide show presentation. Add interesting visuals, and use a color scheme appropriate to the type of business you choose. Use a chart to show how well the company has performed. Add a table to one of the slides.

b. Use slide transitions, animation effects, and slide timings. Remember, your audience consists of a group of advertising executives who create eye-catching ads every day. View the slide show to evaluate the effects you added.

c. Add your name as a footer to slides and handouts. Spell check and save the presentation as "NAAA Presentation" to your Project Disk. Print it as handouts, six slides per page.

3. You are the manager of the Maryland University Student Employment Office. The office is staffed by work-study students; new, untrained students start work every semester. Create a presentation that you can use to make the training easier. You can create your own content, or use the following: the work-study staff needs to learn about the main features of the office, including its employment database, library of company directories, seminars on employment search strategies, interviewing techniques, and resume development, as well as its student consulting and resume bulk-mailing services.

To complete this independent challenge:

a. Plan and create the slide presentation. Use Microsoft Clip Gallery to help create visual interest.

b. Save the presentation as "Student Employment" to your Project Disk. View the slide show and evaluate the contents of your presentation. Make any necessary adjustments.

c. Add transitions, special effects, and timings to the presentation. Remember, your audience is university students who need to assimilate a lot of information in order to perform well in their new jobs. View the slide show again.

d. Add your name as a footer to slides and handouts. Spell check, save, and print the presentation.

4. MediaLoft gives monthly Brown Bag seminars during lunchtime to interested employees. MediaLoft has asked Asset Advisors, a successful investment service company, to give a Brown Bag presentation on sound investment principles. You work for Asset Advisors, and your manager, Kevin Leong, has asked you to prepare the presentation for the MediaLoft session. He knows that MediaLoft's corporate values include socially responsible investing, so Kevin has asked you to include something in the presentation about this topic.

To complete this independent challenge:

a. Open the file PPT D-6 from your Project Disk, and save it as "Investment Presentation" to your Project Disk.

b. Look through the presentation and adjust the content as necessary. Add clip art if you like.

c. Create a Graph chart and embed it on slide 7. Enter the data in Table D-6 into the datasheet.

d. Format the chart, and title the chart "Investment Risk Over Time."

e. Format the objects in the presentation. Use the Align and Group commands to organize the shapes.

f. Connect to the Internet, go to the MediaLoft intranet site at http://www.course.com/illustrated/MediaLoft and click the Research Center link. From there, click the Socially Responsible Investing link, and examine the sites listed there and some of the sites listed within them. Create two new slides in your presentation, one about organizations that promote socially responsible investing and another about investment funds that invest only in socially responsible organizations.

g. Fill in the appropriate information on the last two slides in the presentation.

h. Make changes to the color scheme and add the new color scheme to the color scheme list. Change the slide background to a 2-color background with the gradient of your choice.

i. Spell check the presentation and evaluate the presentation. Set appropriate animations, slide transitions, and slide timings. View the slide show again.

j. Add your name as a footer to slides and handouts. Save the presentation and print the slides, six handouts per page. Close the presentation and disconnect from the Internet.

TABLE D-6

	1 year	3 year	5 year	10 year
Bonds	8.2%	7.5%	5.6%	2.9%
Stocks	17.3%	8.9%	6.1%	3.2%
Mutual Funds	15.4%	6.1%	5.2%	4.7%

PowerPoint 2000

▶ Visual Workshop

Create a slide that looks like the example in Figure D-22. Add your name as a footer on the slide. Save the presentation as "Costs" to your Project Disk.

FIGURE D-22

PowerPoint 2000

Unit E

Customizing
Your Presentation

Objectives

► **Understand PowerPoint masters**
[MOUS] ► **Format master text**
[MOUS] ► **Change master text indents**
► **Adjust text objects**
► **Use advanced drawing tools**
[MOUS] ► **Use advanced formatting tools**
► **Use the Style Checker**
[MOUS] ► **Create and customize a Toolbar**

Design features such as text spacing and color are some of the most important qualities of a professional-looking presentation. It is important, however, to make design elements consistent throughout a presentation to hold the reader's attention and to avoid confusion. PowerPoint helps you achieve the look you want by providing ways to customize and enhance your slides, notes pages, and handouts. ◄— Maria Abbott, the general sales manager of MediaLoft, is working on a presentation that she will give at a meeting of store managers. After receiving feedback from the coworkers, she revises her presentation by customizing the format of her slides and enhancing the graphics.

Understanding PowerPoint Masters

Presentations in PowerPoint use **Slide Masters**, templates for all of the slides in the presentation. Three of the PowerPoint views have a corresponding master view—Slide Master view for Slide view, Notes Master view for Notes Page view, and Handout Master view for Slide Sorter view. Slide view actually has two masters; the second, called the Title Master, allows you to customize just the title slide of your presentation. Design elements that you place on the Slide Master appear on every slide in the presentation. When you insert an object or change text formatting in one of the text placeholders on the Slide Master, the change appears in all the slides of the presentation. For example, you could insert a company logo in the upper-right corner of the Slide Master and that logo would then appear on every slide in your presentation. When you apply a template from another presentation, the Slide Masters from that presentation automatically replace the existing ones. You can always override the settings on the Slide Master by changing the background, text formats, and color scheme in the Slide pane or Slide view, then clicking Apply in the dialog box. As long as you click Apply, not Apply All, the changes will affect only the displayed slide. ◢━━━━ Maria wants to make a few changes to the presentation design, so she opens her presentation and examines the Slide Master.

QuickTip

To return personalized tool-bars and menus to the default state, click Tools on the menu bar, click Customize, click Reset my usage data on the Options tab, click Yes, then click Close.

1. Start PowerPoint, open the presentation **PPT E-1**, then save it as **1999 Sales Presentation 3**
   The title slide of the presentation appears.

2. Click **Window** on the menu bar, then click **Arrange All**
   This ensures that your screen will match the figures in this book.

3. Click **View**, point to **Master**, then click **Title Master**
   The presentation's Title Master appears, showing the master elements along with the Master toolbar. A slide miniature may also appear.

QuickTip

You can also hold down [Shift] and click the Slide View button ▭ to display the slide master.

4. Drag the **vertical scroll box** to the top of the scroll bar, then, if the slide miniature is visible, click the **Close box** ✕ on the slide miniature
   The Slide Master appears. It contains a **Master title placeholder**, and a **Master text placeholder** as shown in Figure E-1. These placeholders control the format for each title text object and main text object for each slide in the presentation after slide 1. Figure E-2 shows slide 2 of the presentation. Examine Figures E-1 and E-2 to better understand the relationship between the Slide Master and the slide.

QuickTip

In Slide Master view, click New Title Master on the Common Tasks menu button to add a Title Master to a presentation that does not have one.

   - The Master title placeholder, labeled "Title Area for AutoLayouts," indicates the position of the title text object and its font size, style, and color. Compare this to the slide title shown in Figure E-2.
   - The Master text placeholder, labeled "Object Area for AutoLayouts" determines the characteristics of the main text objects on all the slides in the presentation. Notice how the bullet levels in the main text object of Figure E-2 compare to the corresponding bullet levels of the Master text placeholder in Figure E-1.
   - You can resize and move master title and text placeholders as you would any placeholder in PowerPoint.
   - Slide Masters can also contain background objects, such AutoShapes, clip art, or pictures that will appear on every slide in the presentation behind the text and objects you place on the slides. In Maria's presentation, the company logo appears on both the Title Master and the Slide Master, so that it shows on every slide in the presentation.

FIGURE E-1: Slide Master

Master toolbar

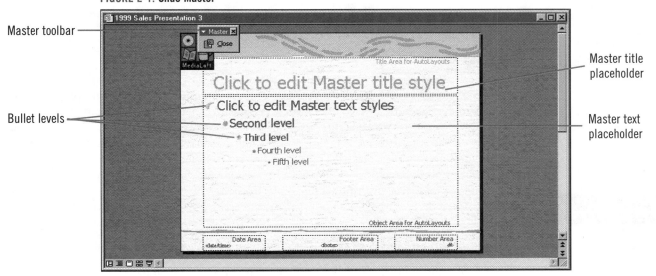

Master title placeholder

Bullet levels

Master text placeholder

FIGURE E-2: Slide 2 in Slide view

Title text object

Main text object

PowerPoint 2000

Changing the Master Layout

When you are in Slide Master or Title Master view, the Slide Layout command on the Common Tasks toolbar changes to Master Layout. Clicking Master Layout opens the Master Layout dialog box, as shown in Figure E-3. If you happen to delete a master placeholder or if one doesn't appear in a master view, use the Master Layout dialog box to reapply a master placeholder. Each master view has its own Master Layout dialog box.

FIGURE E-3: Master Layout dialog box

Formatting Master Text

Formatting text in a master view works the same as it does in other views, but PowerPoint applies the changes you make to the whole presentation. This ensures that you don't use a mixture of fonts and styles throughout the presentation. For example, if your presentation is part of a marketing campaign for a travel tour to the Middle East, you may decide to switch the title text font of the entire presentation from the standard Times New Roman font to a script font. You can change text color, style, size, and bullet type in the master view. When you change a bullet type, you can use a character bullet symbol from a font, a picture bullet from the Clip Gallery, or an image that you scan in. ⬤━ Maria decides to make a few formatting changes to the text of her Slide Master.

Steps

1. Make sure the Slide Master is still visible

2. Move I anywhere in the first line of text in the Master text placeholder, then click
   The insertion point appears. To make the formatting changes to the whole line of text, you don't have to select the line; just click to insert the insertion point. The first line of text could be more prominent.

Trouble?

If you don't see the Text Shadow button, click the More Buttons button 🔢 on the Formatting toolbar.

3. Click the **Bold button** **B** on the Formatting toolbar, then click the **Text Shadow button** **S** on the Formatting toolbar
   The first line of text becomes bold with a shadow. The third level bullet would be more visible if it were darker.

4. Right-click anywhere in the third line of text in the Master text placeholder, then click **Bullets and Numbering** on the pop-up menu
   The Bullets and Numbering dialog box opens. Notice that there is also a Numbered tab that you can use to create sequentially numbered or lettered bullets.

QuickTip

A bullet looks best if it is the same size or smaller than the text it identifies. Use the Size spin arrows to specify the percentage of the text size you want the bullet to be.

5. Click **Character**, click the **Bullets from list arrow**, then click **Wingdings**
   The available bullet choices change.

6. Click the **airplane** in the second row, as shown in Figure E-4, click the **Color list arrow**, then click the **blue-gray square** (labeled Follow Shadows Scheme Color)

7. Click **OK**, then click a blank area of the slide
   A blue-gray airplane replaces the third level bullet.

QuickTip

The first level bullet is a picture bullet. To insert a picture bullet, click Picture in the Bullets and Numbering dialog box, then click the desired bullet. You may need access to the Office 2000 CD to use picture bullets.

8. Click the **Slide View button** 🔲, then click the **slide icon** ▭ for slide 2 in the Outline pane
   Compare your screen to Figure E-5.

9. Click the **Save button** 💾 on the Standard toolbar to save your changes

FIGURE E-4: Bullet dialog box

Choose this
bullet style

FIGURE E-5: Slide 2 with modified text style and bullet type

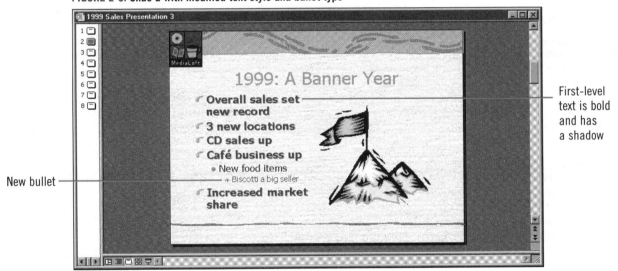

First-level
text is bold
and has
a shadow

New bullet

Applying a template from another presentation

When you apply a template from another presentation, you automatically apply the master layouts, fonts, and colors to the new presentation. To apply a template from another presentation, click the Common Tasks menu button on the Formatting toolbar and click Apply Design template. In the Apply Design Template dialog box, click All Files in the Files of type list box, then use the Look in list arrow to navigate to the presentation whose design you want to apply. (It does not have to be a template.) Click the presentation or template name, then click Apply.

Changing Master Text Indents

The master text placeholder in every presentation has five levels of text, called **indent levels**. You can use the horizontal slide ruler to control the space between the bullets and the text or to change the position of the whole indent level. Each indent level is represented by two small triangles called **indent markers** on the ruler that identify the position of each indent level in the master text placeholder. You can also set tabs on the horizontal ruler by clicking the tab indicator to the left of the horizontal ruler. Table E-1 describes the indent and tab markers on the ruler. ▄▄ Maria decides to change the distance between the bullet symbols and the text in the first two indent levels of her presentation to emphasize the bullets.

1. Click **View** on the menu bar, point to **Master**, then click **Slide Master**
The Slide Master appears.

Trouble?

If your rulers are already visible skip step 2.

2. Click anywhere in the master text placeholder to place the insertion point, click **View** on the menu bar, then click **Ruler**
The rulers and indent markers for the Master text placeholder appear. The indent markers are set so that the first line of text in each level, in this case the bullet, begins to the left of subsequent lines of text. This is a **hanging indent**.

Trouble?

If you accidentally drag an indent marker into another marker. Click the Undo button 🔙 to restore the indent levels to their original position.

3. Position the pointer over the left indent marker △ of the first indent level, then drag to the right to the ½" mark
Compare your screen to Figure E-6.

4. Position the pointer over the left indent marker of the second indent level, then drag to the right to the 1⅛" mark
See Figure E-7. The rulers take up valuable screen area.

QuickTip

You can add tabs to any level text by clicking on the ruler where you want the tab. Click the tab indicator to the left of the ruler to cycle through the different tab alignment options.

5. Click the right mouse button in a blank area of the Presentation window, then click **Ruler** on the pop-up menu
The rulers are no longer visible.

6. Click **Close** on the Master toolbar
Slide Master view closes and slide 2 appears, showing the increased indents in the main text object.

7. Click the **Save button** 💾 on the Standard toolbar

TABLE E-1: Indent and Tab Markers

symbol	name	function
▽	First line indent marker	Controls the position of the first line of text in an indent level
△	Left indent marker	Controls the position of subsequent lines of text in an indent level
▢	Margin marker	Moves both indent markers of an indent level at the same time
⌊	Left aligned tab	Aligns tab text on the left
⌋	Right aligned tab	Aligns tab text on the right
⊥	Center aligned tab	Aligns tab text in the center
⊥	Decimal aligned tab	Aligns tab text on a decimal point

FIGURE E-6: Slide Master with first-level, left, indent marker moved

First-line indent marker

Left indent marker

Horizontal ruler

FIGURE E-7: Slide Master with second-level, left, indent marker moved

Second-level left indent marker moved

Second-level indent increased

Exceptions to the Slide Master

If you change the format of text on a slide and then apply a different template to the presentation, the slide that you formatted retains the text formatting changes you made. These format changes that differ from the Slide Master are known as **exceptions**. Exceptions can only be changed on the individual slides where they occur. For example, you might change the font and size of a particular piece of text on a slide to make it stand out and then decide later to add a different template to your presentation. The text you formatted before you applied the template is an exception, and it is unaffected by the new template. Another way to override the slide master is to remove the master graphics on one or more slides. You might want to do this to get a clearer view of your slide text. Click Format on the menu bar, click Background, then click the Omit background graphics from master check box to select it.

Adjusting Text Objects

You have complete control over the placement of your text in PowerPoint. With the **text anchor** feature, you can adjust text position within text objects or shapes to achieve the best look. If you want your text to fill more or less of the slide, you can adjust the spacing between lines of text, called **leading** (rhymes with "wedding"). ✎ Maria decides that the graphic on the last slide in her presentation makes it look cluttered. She decides to delete it and adjust the text position and line spacing to give the slide a more open and polished look.

Steps

1. Drag the **vertical scroll box** down to view slide 8

2. Click the **graphic**, then press **[Delete]**

3. Click the **Common Tasks menu button** on the Formatting toolbar, click **Slide Layout**, select the **Bulleted List AutoLayout**, then click **Apply**

4. Press **[Shift]**, right-click the **main text object**, click **Format Placeholder** on the pop-up menu, then click the **Text Box tab**
   The Format AutoShape dialog box opens, similar to Figure E-8. The text would look better centered in the text box.

5. Click the **Text anchor point list arrow**, click **Top Centered**, then click **OK**
   The text moves to the center of the text object. The bullets are a little too close together.

6. Click **Format** on the menu bar, then click **Line Spacing**
   The Line Spacing dialog box opens, similar to Figure E-9.

7. In the After paragraph section, click the **up spin arrow** three times so that 0.15 appears, click **Preview**, then drag the dialog box out of the way
   The space, or leading, after each paragraph increases, and the text automatically becomes smaller to make it look less crowded.

8. In the Line spacing section, click the **up spin arrow** twice so that 1.1 appears, then click **Preview**
   The line spacing between the text lines increases and the text shrinks again. Because each bulleted item is considered to be a separate paragraph, the Line Spacing and the After Paragraph commands have similar effects.

9. Click **OK**, then click in a blank area of the Presentation window to deselect the main text object
   Compare your screen to Figure E-10.

FIGURE E-8: Format AutoShape dialog box

Click to change the text anchor point

FIGURE E-9: Line Spacing dialog box

Step 8

Step 7

FIGURE E-10: Slide showing formatted main text object

CLUES TO USE

Changing margins around text in shapes

You can also use the Text Anchor Point command to change the margins around a text object to form a shape that suits the text better. Right-click the shape, click Format Placeholder, click the Text Box tab, then adjust the Internal margin settings. Click Preview to see your changes before you apply them to the shape.

Using Advanced Drawing Tools

PowerPoint has a number of powerful drawing tools on the AutoShapes menu to help you draw all types of shapes. For example, the Curve drawing tool allows you to create a freeform curved line, the Arc tool helps you draw smooth, curved lines and pie-shaped wedges, and the Connector line tool allows you to connect slide objects with a line. Once you have drawn a shape, you can format and rearrange it to create the effect you want. ✏️ Maria uses the Arc tool and a Connector line tool to complete the diagram on slide 7.

Steps 1 2 3 4

1. Click the **slide icon** ☐ for slide 7, click the **AutoShapes menu button** on the Drawing toolbar, point to **Basic Shapes**, then click the **Arc button** ◥
The pointer changes to ✛.

2. Position ✛ on the center of the left edge of the **CDs object**, then drag down to the top, center edge of the **Videos object**
See Figure E-11. The direction in which you drag the arc determines whether the arc opens up or down and the distance you drag the arc determines its size.

   QuickTip
   To constrain the arc to a proportional size, press and hold edge down [Shift] while you drag.

3. Drag the arc's **bottom adjustment handle** down and to the right so the arc becomes a half circle, then drag the lower middle sizing handle down so that the end of the arc touches the middle of the Books object
The adjustment handle determines the length of the arc; the sizing handle changes its size.

4. Click the **Line Style button** ≡ on the Drawing toolbar, then click the **4½ pt** line style
The line style of the arc changes to a thicker weight.

5. Click the **Arrow Style button** ⇄ on the Drawing toolbar, then click **Arrow Style 5**
An arrowhead appears on the arc. The direction in which you dragged the arc determines the direction of the arrowhead. The arrow is in front of the Videos object.

   QuickTip
   To change the default attributes of a particular AutoShape, format the AutoShape, select it, click Draw on the Drawing toolbar, then click Set AutoShape Defaults.

6. Click the **Draw menu button** on the Drawing toolbar, point to **Order**, click **Send to Back**, then click a blank area of the slide
There needs to be a connector between the Videos and the Café objects.

7. Click the **AutoShapes menu button** on the Drawing toolbar, point to **Connectors**, then click the **Straight Double-Arrow Connector button** ◥

8. Move ✛ to the right side of the **Videos object** until it changes to ⬦ and blue dots appear around the object, then click the blue dot on the right side of the Videos object
The blue dots are anchor points for the connector line.

   Trouble?
   If a green box appears at either end of the line, drag the green square until the blue connection point on the object appears.

9. Move the pointer to the **Café object**, then when you see the blue dot inside the pointer, click the button again to place the right side of the connector line
A red square appears at either end of the connector line, indicating that the line connects the two objects.

10. Click ≡, click **4½ pt**, click in a blank area of the Presentation window, then save the presentation.
Compare your screen to Figure E-12.

FIGURE E-11: **Slide showing drawn arc object**

Adjustment handle

Sizing handle

FIGURE E-12: **Slide showing formatted arc and connector line**

Connector line

Arc

Drawing a freeform shape

A **freeform** shape can consist of straight lines, freehand (or curved) lines, or a combination of the two. To draw a freeform shape, click the AutoShapes menu button, point to Lines, then click the Freeform button. Drag the mouse to draw the desired shape (the cursor changes to a pencil as you draw), then double-click when you are done. To draw a straight line with the Freeform tool, click where you want to begin the line, move the mouse, then double-click to deactivate the Freeform tool. To edit a freeform object, right-click the object, then click Edit Points on the pop-up menu.

PowerPoint 2000

Using Advanced Formatting Tools

PowerPoint 2000

With PowerPoint's advanced formatting tools, you can change formatting attributes such as fill texture, 3-D effects, and shadow for text and shapes. If you like the attributes of an object, you can use the Format Painter button to pick up the attributes and apply them to another object. Maria wants to use the advanced formatting tools to enhance the diagram on the slide.

Steps

1. Right-click the Videos object, click **Format AutoShape** on the pop-up menu, click the **Colors and Lines tab**, click the **Color list arrow** in the Fill section, then click **Fill Effects**
   The Fill Effects dialog box opens.

2. Click the **Texture tab**, click the **down scroll arrow** once, click the **Papyrus square** (first square in the bottom row), click **OK**, then click **OK** again
   The papyrus pattern fills the shape.

3. Click the **3-D button** on the Drawing toolbar, then click **3-D Settings**
   The 3-D Settings toolbar appears.

> **QuickTip**
> When you click the 3-D button on the Drawing toolbar, you can click one of the 3-D styles on the pop-up menu. The default 3-D style is Style 1, the first style in the first row.

4. Click the **Depth button** on the 3-D Settings toolbar, then click **72 pt**.
   A 3-D effect is applied and the depth of the 3-D effect lengthens from the default of 36 points.

5. Click the **Direction button** on the 3-D Settings toolbar, click the right effect in the bottom row, then click the **Close button** on the 3-D Settings toolbar
   The 3-D effect changes to the left side of the object.

6. With the cube still selected, click the **Font Color list arrow** on the Drawing toolbar, then click the **blue square** (third from the left) labeled Follow Shadows Scheme Color
   The other three cube objects would look better if they matched the one you just formatted.

> **QuickTip**
> If you don't see the Format Painter button, try clicking the More Buttons button on the Standard toolbar.

7. Double-click the **Format Painter button** on the Standard toolbar, click each of the other three boxes, then click again to turn off the Format Painter
   Now all the objects on the slide have the same fill effect. When you use the Format Painter tool, it "picks up" the attributes of the object that is selected and copies them to the next object that you click. If you click the Format Painter button only once, it pastes the attributes of the selected object to the next object you select, then turns off automatically. The Books cube is now on top of the arrowhead.

8. Click the **Books cube**, click the **Draw menu button** on the Drawing toolbar, point to **Order**, click **Send to Back**, then click in a blank area of the slide
   Compare your screen to Figure E-13.

9. Press **[Ctrl][Home]** to move to slide 1, click the **Slide Show button**, press **[Spacebar]** or click the left mouse button to run through the presentation, then click the **Slide Sorter View button**
   Compare your screen to Figure E-14.

FIGURE E-13: Slide showing formatted objects

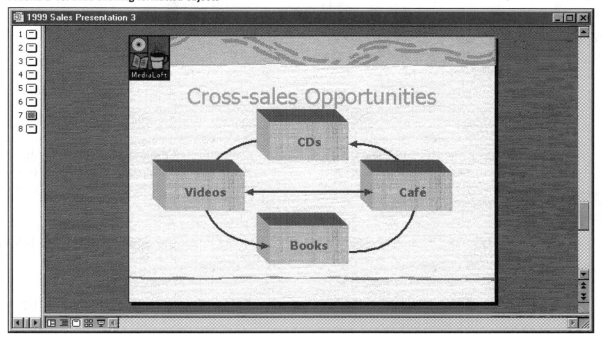

FIGURE E-14: Final presentation in Slide Sorter view

CLUES TO USE

Applying a color scheme to another presentation

If you develop a custom color scheme that you like, you can use the Format Painter tool to apply it to another presentation. To apply a color scheme from one presentation to another, open each presentation in Slide Sorter view, then use the Arrange All command on the Windows menu to arrange the

Presentation windows side by side. Select a slide in the presentation with the color scheme you want to copy, double-click the Format Painter button on the Standard toolbar, then click each slide that you want to change in the other presentation.

Using the Style Checker

To help you correct common design mistakes, the Style Checker feature in PowerPoint reviews your presentation for typical errors such as incorrect font sizes, use of too many fonts, extra words, errors in punctuation, and other readability problems. The Style Checker then suggests ways to improve your presentation. By default, PowerPoint checks your presentation for style inconsistencies and flags potential problem areas with a lightbulb. If you see the lightbulb, click it to see a list of options for handling the problem. ◢▬▬ Maria knows it's easy to overlook mistakes while preparing a presentation, so she reviews the Style Checker settings, then looks for errors she may have missed.

Steps 1 2 3 4

1. Click **Tools** on the menu bar, click **Options**, click the **Spelling and Style tab** in the Options dialog box, then click **Style Options**
   The Style Options dialog box opens, similar to Figure E-15.

2. Click check boxes as necessary so that your screen matches the dialog box shown in Figure E-15

3. Click the **Visual Clarity tab**, click **Defaults**, then review the options
   The Style Checker Options dialog box indicates the current option settings for visual clarity.

4. Click **OK** twice

5. Click **Help** on the menu bar, then click **Show the Office Assistant**
   The Office Assistant appears. It may display several tips for working with your presentation.

6. Click **slide 8**, click the **Slide View button** ▣, then click the **lightbulb** on slide 8
   The Office Assistant tells you that the text in the main text placeholder should use sentence case capitalization, in other words, that only the first letter in each bulleted item should be capital. See Figure E-16. You know this is not a problem.

7. Click **OK** to ignore this message, then click the **lightbulb** that appears at the bottom of the slide
   Now the Office Assistant tells you that you have too much text on this slide. This layout is fine for the Thank You slide.

8. Click **OK**

9. Go to **slide 4**, click the **lightbulb** on the slide, then click **OK** to ignore the capitalization suggestions

10. Hide the Office Assistant again, then save your changes

FIGURE E-15: Case and End Punctuation tab in the Style Options dialog box

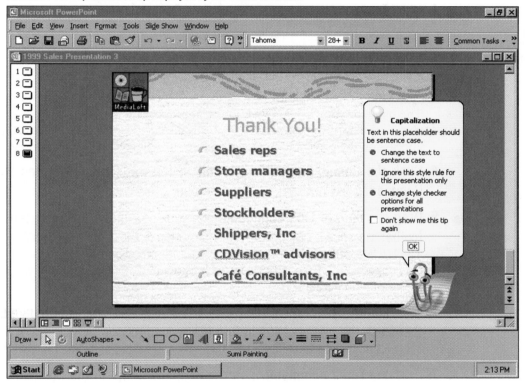

FIGURE E-16: Capitalization tip displayed by the Office Assistant

Understanding Style Checker options

The Style Checker is helpful, but before you accept its suggestions, be careful that it doesn't make changes you don't expect. In the Capitalization tip, for example, if you had selected the "Change the text to sentence case" option, all the uppercase letters in the middle of each bullet would become lowercase. In the "Too much text" warning shown in Figure E-17, the first two options would add slides to your presentation.

FIGURE E-17: "Too much text" warning

Creating and Customizing a Toolbar

PowerPoint 2000

As you know from working with PowerPoint, the program automatically customizes toolbars based on how often you use the buttons. You can use the Customize command on the Tools menu to add and remove buttons so they contain only the buttons you want. You can also create your own toolbars that contain only the menu commands and images you select, giving you easy access to program features you use frequently in your particular work situation. Maria creates a custom toolbar to help her update and view the links in her presentation and then modifies it by adding buttons and images to suit her needs.

QuickTip
You can also right-click any toolbar, then click Customize on the pop-up menu.

1. Click **Tools** on the menu bar, then click **Customize**.
   The Customize dialog box opens.

2. Click the **Toolbars tab**, then click **New**
   The New Toolbar dialog box opens, asking you to name your new toolbar.

3. Type **Links**, then click **OK**
   The name of your new toolbar, Links, appears at the bottom of the toolbars list. It has a check mark next to it, indicating that it is displayed on the screen. A small, empty toolbar appears on the presentation screen next to the dialog box, as shown in Figure E-18.

4. Click the **Commands tab**, click **Edit** in the Categories list, then scroll down the Commands list until you see Update Link

QuickTip
You can drag any command from the Commands list to *any* toolbar displayed on your screen.

5. Drag the **Update Link command** over your new menu until you see I on the Links toolbar, as shown in Figure E-19, then release the mouse button
   The Update Link command appears in your new toolbar. For commands that don't have an icon already associated with them, such as the Links commands, you can add a graphic to the command name.

6. Click **Modify Selection** in the Customize dialog box, point to **Change Button Image**, then click the image of the **bell** in the second row
   The bell image is added to the left of the command name on the toolbar.

QuickTip
To remove a button from a toolbar, open the Customize dialog box, then drag the button off the toolbar.

7. Drag the **Links command** from the Commands list in the Customize dialog box to the right of the Update Link command on the Links toolbar, then change the button image to include the **telephone image**
   See Figure E-20.

8. Click the **Toolbars** tab
   If you are working in a lab, you may not be able to create new toolbars, so it's best to delete them.

9. Make sure the **Links toolbar** is selected (not just the check box next to it), click **Delete**, click **OK** in the alert box, then click **Close** in the Customize dialog box
   The new toolbar disappears from the screen.

10. Add your name in the notes and handouts footer, save your changes, print the presentation as **Handouts (6 per page)** in pure black and white, close the presentation, and exit PowerPoint

FIGURE E-18: New custom toolbar

New toolbar
(currently empty)

FIGURE E-19: Dragging the Update Link command to the custom toolbar

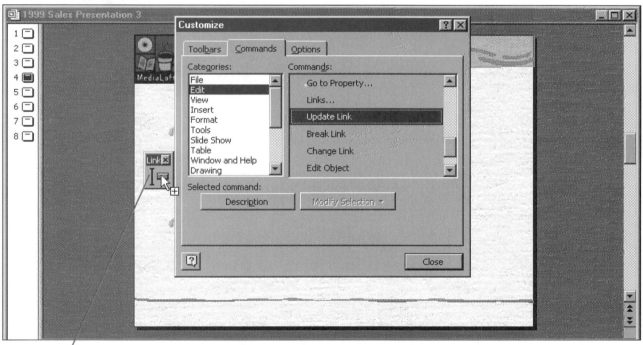

Insertion point indicates
location of new button

FIGURE E-20: Completed toolbar with commands and images

Practice

▶ Concepts Review

Label each of the elements of the PowerPoint window shown in Figure E-21.

FIGURE E-21

Match each of the terms with the statement that describes its function.

10. **Line spacing**
11. **Indent levels**
12. **Text anchor**
13. **Margin marker**
14. **Master**
15. **Bottom indent marker**

a. The five levels of text in a master text placeholder
b. Moves the whole indent level
c. Controls subsequent lines of text in an indent level
d. A template for all the slides in a presentation
e. Adjusts the distance between text lines
f. Adjusts the position of text in a text object

Select the best answer from the list of choices.

16. A hanging indent is an indent in which the
   a. First line of text begins to the right of subsequent lines of text.
   b. First line of text begins to the left of subsequent lines of text.
   c. The bullet symbol is to the left of the first line of text.
   d. The bullet symbol is to the right of the first line of text.

17. A background item on the Title Master
   a. Changes all views of your presentation.
   b. Is only visible on the title slide.
   c. Is a simple way to place an object on every slide of your presentation.
   d. Does not affect the slides of your presentation.

18. The Style Checker checks for all of the following *except*:
   a. Case and punctuation
   b. The number of fonts in a presentation
   c. The number of bullets in a presentation
   d. Incorrect color scheme colors

19. What is leading?
   a. Vertical space between lines of text
   b. Horizontal space between letters
   c. Diagonal space between letters
   d. Space between graphics on the slide master

20. In PowerPoint, tabs
   a. Can be aligned on the left, right, or center of a character or on a decimal.
   b. Determine the location of margins.
   c. Have symbols for top and bottom tabs.
   d. Can be only left or center aligned.

21. When you create a custom toolbar,
   a. You can only have one button on it.
   b. All commands you place there have default graphics.
   c. You can add commands and choose images that represent them.
   d. You can delete it by dragging it off the screen.

▶ Skills Review

1. Format master text.
   a. Start PowerPoint and open the presentation PPT E-2, then save it as "Book Presentation."
   b. Apply the presentation design from PPT E-3. (*Hint:* Remember to select All Files in the Files of type list box and select the folder containing your Project Files in the Look in list box.)
   c. Go to slide 2, switch to Slide Master view, then make the highest level bulleted item in the Master text place-holder bold.
   d. Change the bullet symbol of the highest level bullet to a character bullet in Wingdings 3, the third bullet from the right in the third row, at 75% the size of the text.

    e. Change the bullet color to the dark red color on the far right of the color pop-up menu (named Follow Accent and Followed Hyperlink Scheme Color).

    f. Italicize the second-level bulleted item and change its font to Arial.

    g. Save the presentation.

2. Change master text indents.

    a. Display the rulers.

    b. Move the left indent marker of the first-level bullet to ½" and the second level bullet to 1".

    c. Hide the rulers, switch to Slide view, then save the presentation.

3. Adjust text objects.

    a. Right-click anywhere in the main text object on slide 2, then click Format Placeholder on the pop-up menu.

    b. Click the Text Box tab.

    c. Set the text anchor point to Top Centered.

    d. Adjust the internal margin on all sides to .5 and preview your change.

    e. Select the Resize AutoShape to fit text command, preview it, and click OK.

    f. Select the entire text object. (*Hint:* Press [Shift] while clicking the object.)

    g. Change the line spacing to .75, preview it, then click OK.

    h. Move the text object up about ½".

    i. Save the changes.

4. Use advanced drawing tools.

    a. Go to slide 4.

    b. Use the Elbow Connector to connect the left corner of the Warehouse diamond to the top corner of the MediaLoft Regional Warehouse diamond.

    c. Use the Straight Connector to connect the right side of the Warehouse diamond to the left side of the Individual Stores diamond.

    d. Use the Elbow Arrow Connector to connect the right corner of the Individual Stores diamond to the right corner of the MediaLoft Regional Warehouse diamond.

    e. Select all three of the connector lines, make them 3 points wide, then deselect them.

    f. Apply Arrow Style 5 to the connector line connecting the Individual Stores diamond to the MediaLoft Regional Warehouse diamond.

    g. Deselect all objects, then save your changes.

5. Use advanced formatting tools.

    a. Go to slide 1.

    b. Select the entire text object in the lower-right corner of the slide.

    c. Use the Texture tab in the Fill Effects dialog box to apply the Stationery texture to the object. (*Hint:* Read the description of the selected texture in the box under the textures.)

    d. Double-click the Format Painter to pick up the format of the selected text box on the title slide and apply it to each of the diamond objects on slide 4, then deselect the Format Painter and all objects.

    e. On the title slide, apply the 3-D Style 2 effect to the 1999 Fiscal Year text box.

    f. Use 3-D Settings to change the depth to 72 points and to change the direction so it points in the opposite direction.

    g. Move the text box so it is just inside the lower-right corner of the slide, then close the 3-D Settings toolbar.

    h. Deselect all objects, then save your changes.

6. Use the Style Checker.

   a. Open the Style Options dialog box, and on the Visual Clarity tab, make sure there is a check mark next to the Title text size should be at least, select 48 from the list, then click OK twice.

   b. Turn on the Office Assistant, click in the Presentation window if the Office Assistant displays a tip, then click the lightbulb on the title slide. Notice that the title text font is too small based on your adjustment to the style options.

   c. In the Office Assistant dialog balloon, click Change text to be at least 48 point.

   d. Scroll through the presentation clicking the lightbulbs that appear on the screen. Decide whether to accept the Office Assistant's suggestions or to ignore them. (On slide 5, if the Style Checker offers to find appropriate clip art for the concept of demanding, ignore it by clicking OK.)

   e. Hide the Office Assistant.

7. Create and customize a toolbar.

   a. Create a custom toolbar called "My Toolbar."

   b. Add the Find and Replace commands from the Edit category.

   c. Add the right arrow graphic to the Find button and the down arrow graphic to the Replace button. Notice that they replace the existing graphics.

   d. Drag the Replace button off My Toolbar.

   e. Delete the toolbar named My Toolbar.

   f. Add your name to the footer in the notes and handouts, save the presentation, then print the presentation as handouts, 6 slides per page.

   g. Close the presentation and exit PowerPoint.

▶ Independent Challenges

1. You are the owner of Premier Catering in New York City. You have built your business on banquets, private parties, wedding receptions, and special events over the last five years. To expand, you decide to cater to the local business community by offering executive meals and business luncheons. Use PowerPoint to develop a presentation that you can use to gain corporate catering accounts.

In this independent challenge, you will create an outline and modify the look of a presentation. You will create your own material to complete the slides of the presentation. Assume the following about Premier Catering:

• Premier Catering has eight full-time employees and 10 part-time employees.
• Premier Catering handles catering jobs from 10 to 1000 people.
• Premier Catering is a full-service catering business providing cost estimates, setup, complete preparation, service personnel, and cleanup.

To complete this independent challenge:

   a. Open the file PPT E-4, then save it as "Premier."

   b. Switch to Outline view and create a presentation outline.

   c. Customize your presentation by formatting the Slide Master.

   d. Use PowerPoint's advanced drawing and formatting tools to give your presentation a unique look.

   e. Switch to the last slide and change the text anchor and line spacing to create the best look.

   f. Review the Style Checker options and then check the style of the presentation.

   g. Add your name to the notes and handouts footer, save the presentation, then print the slides of your final presentation as handouts.

2. You are the finance director at Splat Records in Los Angeles, California. Splat Records specializes in alternative music. As an emerging record company, your business is looking for investment capital to expand its talent base and increase sales. It is your responsibility to develop the outline and basic look for a standard presentation that the president can present to various investors.

In this independent challenge, you will complete an outline and choose a custom background for the presentation. You'll need to create a presentation consisting of at least six slides. Assume the following about Splat Records:

- Splat Records has been in business for six years.
- Splat Records currently has 12 recording contracts. Splat wants to double that during the next year and a half.
- Splat Records has two superstar recording groups at the present time: RIM and Blacknight.

    To complete this independent challenge:

a. Open the file PPT E-5, then save it as "Splat."
b. Enter text into the title and main text placeholders of the slides.
c. Use advanced drawing and formatting tools to create a unique look.
d. Check the style of the presentation.
e. Add your name to the notes and handouts footer, save the presentation, then print the slides of your final presentation as handouts in pure black and white.

3. You are the vice president of sales for Redwood Timber Products Inc, a company based in Northern California that harvests redwood trees and sells a number of redwood products. One of your responsibilities is to nurture and develop new business contacts with foreign countries. You are going to give a presentation at an international timber conference in Portland, Oregon, where many prospective foreign buyers will be in attendance.

Plan and create a 10- to 15-slide presentation that focuses on Redwood Timber Products Inc. Redwood Timber Products has been in business for over 75 years and employs a 320-person workforce. Develop your own content, but assume the following:

- Redwood Timber Products harvests 75,000 acres per year and replants 92,000 acres per year.
- Redwood Timber Products can harvest and deliver 400,000 tons of timber per month overseas.
- Redwood Timber Products uses Pacific Shipping Inc to deliver timber to overseas locations.
- Timber prices range from $10 to $16 per board foot depending on the size and grade (or quality) of the lumber. Lumber grades are designated with numbers as follows: "1" for top grade, "2" for middle grade, and "3" for bottom grade.
- Many of the attendees at the conference are from Middle Eastern countries.

The presentation will be shown with a projection screen and will last approximately 30 minutes.
    To complete this independent challenge:

a. Think about the results you want to see, the information you need to create the slide presentation, what type of message you want to communicate, and the target audience.
b. Use the AutoContent Wizard to help you start an outline.
c. Modify the Slide and Title Masters: Modify the text size, change one bullet to a character bullet, and adjust the space between a bullet and the text after it.
d. Use at least one 3-D object and customize its fill, 3-D direction, and depth.
e. Format the content, then save the presentation as "Redwood."
f. Add your name to the notes and handouts footer, save the presentation, then print the final presentation as handouts.

4. You have been a MediaLoft employee for six months and have recently met another employee named Stan. Stan enjoys working at MediaLoft but also has a talent for creating computer games. He has asked you to help him market the idea. You talk it over and decide to approach MediaLoft management with the idea of marketing Stan's computer games. You use the MediaLoft intranet site to help you collect marketing information. The site gives employees access to company-wide information. Develop a 10- to 15-slide presentation that promotes the software product idea. Use PowerPoint clip art and shapes to enhance your slides. Use one of PowerPoint's templates, design one of your own, or copy one from another presentation. You can use one of the following three ideas that you and Stan have been developing, or you can develop some of your own.

- "Cavern Adventures," an interactive game in which you lead a group of thrill seekers on one of 10 different cave adventures throughout the world
- "Posse," an interactive game that puts you in one of six different historical situations, where you lead a "posse" of people chasing after a convicted murderer
- "Spies," an adventure game in which you are a spy for the Axis Powers or the Allies during World War II; assume there are six different situations to choose from for each political side

Create your own information, but assume the following:

- The product is designed for adults and children ages 13 and up.
- The cost of product development is estimated to be $250,000. Development time is four months.
- The retail price of the final product is designed to be $50, given the current product development cost estimate. For every $10,000 increase in product development cost, the base retail price goes up $2.

To complete this independent challenge:

a. Plan the story line of how the software was developed using five or more slides. Plan the beginning and ending slides. What do you want your audience to know about the product idea?

b. Use clip art and shapes to enhance the presentation. Change the bullet and text formatting in the master text and title placeholders to fit the subject matter.

c. Use demographic information collected from a recent MediaLoft marketing survey to show how the target audience for your software is the same as MediaLoft's book-buying audience. Connect to the Internet and go to the MediaLoft intranet site at http://www.course.com/illustrated/MediaLoft. Click the Marketing link and use the information on the 1999 Book Survey Results link.

d Save the presentation as "Games."

e. Add your name to the notes and handouts footer, save the presentation, then print the final slide presentation as handouts in pure black and white.

PowerPoint 2000

► Visual Workshop

Create two slides that look like the examples in Figures E-22 and E-23. Be sure to use connector lines. Add your name to the handout footer, then save the presentation as "New Products." Print the Slide view of the presentation. Submit the final presentation output.

FIGURE E-22

FIGURE E-23

PowerPoint 2000 MOUS Certification Objectives

Below is a list of the Microsoft Office User Specialist program objectives for Core PowerPoint 2000 skills showing where each MOUS objective is covered in the Lessons and Practice. This table lists the Core MOUS certification skills covered in the units in this book (Units A-E). The core skills without page references are covered in the Intermediate and Advanced Editions. For more information on which Course Guide—Illustrated titles meet MOUS certification, please see the inside cover of this book.

MOUS standardized coding number	Activity	Lesson page where skill is covered	Location in lesson where skill is covered	Practice
PP2000.1	**Creating a presentation**			
PP2000.1.1	Delete slides	PowerPoint B-8	QuickTip	Skills Review Independent Challenges 1, 2, 4
PP2000.1.2	Create a specified type of slide	PowerPoint B-4 PowerPoint B-8 PowerPoint B-9	Steps 4–5 Steps 1–2 Table B-3	Skills Review, Independent Challenges 1–4, Visual Workshop
PP2000.1.3	Create a presentation from a template and/or a Wizard	PowerPoint B-4	Steps 1–5	Skills Review, Independent Challenges 1–4, Visual Workshop
PP2000.1.4	Navigate among different views (slide, outline, sorter, tri-pane)	PowerPoint A-10	Steps 1–8	Skills Review
PP2000.1.5	Create a new presentation from existing slides	PowerPoint C-2 PowerPoint C-12	Steps 1–9 Clues to Use	Skills Review
PP2000.1.6	Copy a slide from one presentation into another	PowerPoint C-12	Clues to Use	Skills Review
PP2000.1.7	Insert headers and footers	PowerPoint B-13 PowerPoint B-14	Clues to Use Steps 5–7	Skills Review, Independent Challenges 1–4
PP2000.1.8	Create a blank presentation	PowerPoint A-7 PowerPoint B-4	Table A-2 Table B-1	
PP2000.1.9	Create a presentation using the AutoContent Wizard	PowerPoint A-6	Steps 1–8	Skills Review, Independent Challenges 2, 3, Visual Workshop
PP2000.2	**Modifying a presentation**			
PP2000.2.1	Change the order of slides using Slide Sorter view	PowerPoint B-16	Step 3	Skills Review, Independent Challenges 1–4
PP2000.2.2	Find and replace text	PowerPoint C-15	Clues to Use	Skills Review
PP2000.2.3	Change the layout for one or more slides	PowerPoint D-2	Steps 3–4	Skills Review, Independent Challenge 1
PP2000.2.4	Change slide layout (Modify the Slide Master)	PowerPoint E-4 PowerPoint E-6	Steps 1–7 Steps 1–6 Clues to Use	Skills Review, Independent Challenges 1, 3, 4

MOUS standardized coding number	Activity	Lesson page where skill is covered	Location in lesson where skill is covered	Practice
PP2000.2.5	Modify slide sequence in the outline pane	PowerPoint B-10 PowerPoint B-11	QuickTip Table B-4	
PP2000.2.6	Apply a design template	PowerPoint B-4 PowerPoint B-5 PowerPoint B-17	Steps 1–4 Clues to Use Clues to Use	Skills Review
PP2000.3	**Working with text**			
PP2000.3.1	Check spelling	PowerPoint B-14	Steps 1–4	Skills Review, Independent Challenges 1–4
PP2000.3.2	Change and replace text fonts (individual slide and entire presentation)	PowerPoint C-14 PowerPoint C-15	Steps 7–8 Clues to Use	Skills Review, Visual Workshop
PP2000.3.3	Enter text in tripane view	PowerPoint B-6 PowerPoint B-8	Steps 1–7 Steps 1–8	Skills Review
PP2000.3.4	Import text from Word	PowerPoint C-13	Clues to Use	Skills Review
PP2000.3.5	Change the text alignment	PowerPoint C-14	Step 9	Skills Review
PP2000.3.6	Create a text box for entering text	PowerPoint C-12	Steps 2–4 QuickTip	Skills Review, Independent Challenge 3, Visual Workshop
PP2000.3.7	Use the Wrap text in TextBox Autoshape feature	PowerPoint C-12 PowerPoint C-14	Steps 2–4 QuickTip	Skills Review
PP2000.3.8	Use the Office Clipboard	PowerPoint C-7	Clues to Use	
PP2000.3.9	Use the Format Painter	PowerPoint E-12	Step 7	Skills Review
PP2000.3.10	Promote and Demote text in slide & outline panes	PowerPoint B-8 PowerPoint B-10 PowerPoint B-11	Steps 6–9 Steps 4–9 Table B-4	
PP2000.4	**Working with visual elements**			
PP2000.4.1	Add a picture from the Clip Art Gallery	PowerPoint D-2	Steps 4–7	Skills Review, Independent Challenges 1–4
PP2000.4.2	Add and group shapes using WordArt or the Drawing Toolbar	PowerPoint C-4 PowerPoint C-10	Steps 5–6 Steps 1–4	Skills Review
PP2000.4.3	Apply formatting	PowerPoint C-4 PowerPoint C-14	Steps 8–9 Steps 1–9	Skills Review
PP2000.4.4	Place text inside a shape using a text box	PowerPoint C-6	Steps 7–8	Skills Review
PP2000.4.5	Scale and size an object including Clip Art	PowerPoint C-4 PowerPoint C-6 PowerPoint D-2 PowerPoint D-4	Step 7 Steps 1–2 Step 8 Step 8	Unit C–Skills Review Unit D–Skills Review Independent Challenges 3, 4, Visual Workshop

MOUS standardized coding number	Activity	Lesson page where skill is covered	Location in lesson where skill is covered	Practice
PP2000.4.6	Create tables within PowerPoint	PowerPoint D-14	Steps 1–2	Skills Review Independent Challenge
PP2000.4.7	Rotate and fill an object	PowerPoint C-11 PowerPoint C-4	Clues to Use Step 9	Skills Review
PP2000.5	**Customizing a presentation**			
PP2000.5.1	Add AutoNumber bullets	PowerPoint E-4	Step 4	
PP2000.5.2	Add speaker notes	PowerPoint B-12	Steps 1–7	Skills Review, Independent Challenges 1–4
PP2000.5.3	Add graphical bullets	PowerPoint E-4	Step 4–7 Quick Tip	Skills Review, Independent Challenges 1, 3, 4
PP2000.5.4	Add slide transitions	PowerPoint D-16	Steps 1–8	Skills Review, Independent Challenges 1–4
PP2000.5.5	Animate text and objects	PowerPoint D-18	Steps 1–8	Skills Review, Independent Challenges 1–4
PP2000.6	**Creating output**			
PP2000.6.1	Preview presentation in black and white	PowerPoint A-17	Clues to Use	
PP2000.6.2	Print slides in a variety of formats	PowerPoint A-16	Steps 1–7 QuickTip	Skills Review, Independent Challenges 2, 3, Visual Workshop
PP2000.6.3	Print audience handouts	PowerPoint A-16	Steps 3–6	Skills Review, Independent Challenge 2, Visual Workshop
PP2000.6.4	Print speaker notes in a specified format	PowerPoint B-14	Step 9	Skills Review
PP2000.7	**Delivering a presentation**			
PP2000.7.2	Use on-screen navigation tools	PowerPoint D-12	Steps 2–4 Steps 8–9	Skills Review
PP2000.7.3	Print a slide as an overhead transparency	PowerPoint A-16	Quick Tip	Skills Review
PP2000.7.4	Use the pen during a presentation	PowerPoint D-12	Steps 5–7	Skills Review
PP2000.8	**Managing files**			
PP2000.8.1	Save changes to a presentation	PowerPoint A-12	Step 5	Skills Review
PP2000.8.2	Save as a new presentation	PowerPoint A-12	Steps 1–3	Skills Review, Independent Challenges 2, 3, Visual Workshop

MOUS standardized coding number	Activity	Lesson page where skill is covered	Location in lesson where skill is covered	Practice
PP2000.8.4	Use Office Assistant	PowerPoint A-14	Steps 1–9	Skills Review, Independent Challenges 1, 4
PP2000E.1	**Creating a presentation**			
PP2000E.1.3	Design a template	PowerPoint B-17	Clues to Use	Skills Review
PP2000E.2	**Modifying a presentation**			
PP2000E.2.1	Change tab formatting	PowerPoint E-6	Quick Tip Table E-1	
PP2000E.2.2	Use the Wrap text in AutoShape feature	PowerPoint C-12 PowerPoint C-14	Steps 2–4 Quick Tip	Skills Review
PP2000E.2.3	Apply a template from another presentation	PowerPoint B-17	Clues to Use	Skills Review, Independent Challenge 4
PP2000E.2.4	Customize a color scheme	PowerPoint C-16	Steps 1–2 Steps 7–10	Skills Review, Independent Challenges 2, 4
PP2000E.2.5	Apply animation effects	PowerPoint D-18	Steps 1–8	Skills Review, Independent Challenges 1–4
PP2000E.2.6	Create a custom background	PowerPoint C-16	Steps 3–6	Skills Review, Independent Challenges 3, 4
PP2000E.2.9	Customize clip art and other objects (resize, scale, etc.)	PowerPoint C-4 PowerPoint C-6 PowerPoint D-2 PowerPoint D-4	Step 7 Steps 1–2 Step 8 Step 8	Unit C—Skills Review, Independent Challenges 3, 4, Visual Workshop, Unit D—Skills Review
PP2000E.2.13	Set automatic slide timings	PowerPoint D-16	Steps 1–3	Skills Review, Independent Challenges 1–3
PP2000E.3	**Working with visual elements**			
PP2000E.3.1	Add textured backgrounds	PowerPoint E-12	Steps 1–2	Skills Review, Independent Challenges 1, 2
PP2000E.3.2	Apply diagonal borders to a table	PowerPoint D-14	Quick Tip	
PP2000E.5	**Creating output**			
PP2000E.5.1	Save slide as a graphic	PowerPoint D-5	Clues to Use	
PP2000E.5.3	Change output format (Page setup)	PowerPoint A-16	Quick Tip step 7	Skills Review
PP2000E.6	**Delivering a presentation**			
PP2000E.6.3	View a Presentation on the Web	PowerPoint A-23		Independent Challenge 4 Skills Review, Independent Challenges 2–4

MOUS standardized coding number	Activity	Lesson page where skill is covered	Location in lesson where skill is covered	Practice
PP2000E.7	**Managing files**			
PP2000E.7.1	Save embedded fonts in presentation	PowerPoint A-12	Clues to Use	Skills Review
PP2000E.8	**Working with PowerPoint**			
PP2000E.8.1	Customize the toolbar	PowerPoint E-16	Steps 4–9	Skills Review
PP2000E.8.2	Create a toolbar	PowerPoint E-16	Steps 1–3	Skills Review
PP2000E.10	**Working with charts & Tables (Objectives moved from Proficient level)**			
P2000E.10.1	Build a chart or graph	PowerPoint D-6 PowerPoint D-7 PowerPoint D-8	Steps 1–6 Table D-1 Steps 1–9	Skills Review
P2000E.10.2	Modify charts or graphs	PowerPoint D-8 PowerPoint D-9 PowerPoint D-10	Steps 1–9 Clues to Use Steps 1–9 Clues to Use	Skills Review
P2000E.10.5	Modify PowerPoint tables	PowerPoint D-14	Steps 3–10	Skills Review

Glossary

Active cell A selected cell in a Graph datasheet or an Excel worksheet.

Adjustment handle A small diamond positioned next to a sizing handle that changes the dimensions of an object.

Align To place objects' edges or centers on the same plane.

Annotation A freehand drawing on the screen made by using the Annotation tool. You can annotate only in Slide Show view.

AutoContent Wizard A wizard that helps you get your presentation started by supplying a sample outline and a design template.

AutoLayout A predesigned slide layout that contains placeholders for titles, main text, clip art, graphs, and charts.

Background The area behind the text and graphics on a slide.

.bmp The abbreviation for the bitmap graphics file format.

Bullet A small graphic symbol, usually a round or square dot, often used to identify items in a list.

Cell The intersection of a column and row in a worksheet, datasheet, or table.

Chart A graphical representation of information from a datasheet or worksheet. Types include 2-D and 3-D column, bar, pie, area, and line charts.

Clip art Professionally designed pictures that come with PowerPoint.

Clipboard toolbar A toolbar that shows the contents of the Office Clipboard; contains buttons for copying and pasting items to and from the Office Clipboard.

Clip Gallery A library of art, pictures, sounds, video clips, and animations that all Office applications share.

Color scheme The basic eight colors that make up a PowerPoint presentation; a color scheme assigns colors for text, lines, objects, and background color. You can change the color scheme on any presentation at any time.

Common Tasks menu A menu located on the Formatting toolbar that contains commands for common tasks performed in PowerPoint.

Control boxes The gray boxes along the left and top of a Graph datasheet that contain the row and column identifiers.

Crop To hide part of a picture or object using the Cropping tool.

Data label Information that identifies the data in a column or row in a datasheet.

Datasheet The component of a graph that contains the information you want to depict on your Graph chart.

Design templates Prepared slide designs with formatting and color schemes that you can apply to an open presentation.

Dialog box A window that opens when more information is needed to carry out a command.

Drawing toolbar A toolbar that contains buttons that let you create lines and shapes.

Embedded object An object that is created in another application and is copied to a PowerPoint presentation. Embedded objects maintain their identity as files in their original application for easy editing.

File format A file type, such as .wmf or .gif.

Folder A subdivision of a disk that works like a filing system to help you organize files.

Formatting toolbar The toolbar that contains buttons for the most frequently used formatting commands, such as font type and size.

.gif The abbreviation for the graphics interchange format

Graph The program that creates a datasheet and chart to graphically depict information.

Grid Invisible, evenly-spaced horizontal and vertical lines that help you align objects.

Group To combine multiple objects into one object.

Indent levels Text levels in the master text placeholder. Each level is indented a certain amount from the left margin. You control their placement by dragging indent markers on the ruler.

Indent markers Small triangles on the ruler that indicate the location of indent levels, which determine how far text is indented from the left.

Keyword A word you use to quickly find an object.

Leading The spacing between lines of text in a text object.

Main text Sub-points or bullet points on a slide under the slide title.

Main text placeholder A reserved box on a slide for the main text points.

Master text placeholder The placeholder on the Slide Master that controls the formatting and placement of the Main text placeholder on each slide. If you modify the Master text placeholder, each Main text placeholder is affected in the entire presentation.

Master title placeholder The placeholder on the Slide Master that controls the formatting and placement of the Title placeholder on each slide. If you modify the Master title placeholder, each Title placeholder is affected in the entire presentation.

Menu bar The bar beneath the title bar that contains menus that list the program's commands.

More Buttons button A button you click to view toolbar buttons that are not currently visible.

Movie Live action captured in digital format.

Normal view A presentation view that divides the presentation window into Outline, Slide, and Notes panes.

Notes pane In Normal view, the pane that shows speaker notes for the current slide; also in Notes Page view, the area below the slide image that contains speaker notes.

Object The component you place or draw on a slide. Objects are drawn lines and shapes, text, clip art, imported pictures, and embedded objects.

Office Assistant An animated character that appears to offer tips, answer questions, and provide access to the program's Help system.

Office Clipboard A temporary storage area shared by all Office programs that can be used to cut, copy and paste multiple items within and between Office programs. The Office Clipboard can hold up to 12 items collected from any Office program. See also *Clipboard toolbar*.

Organization chart A diagram of connected boxes that shows reporting structure in a company or organization.

Outline pane The presentation window section that shows presentation text in the form of an outline with a small slide icon representing each slide.

Outline view A presentation view that lists the titles and main text of all the slides in your presentation. Also shows a small version of the current slide.

Outlining toolbar The toolbar that contains buttons for the most-used outlining commands, such as moving and indenting text lines.

Pane A section of the presentation window, such as the Outline or Slide pane.

Placeholder A dashed line box where you place text or objects.

PowerPoint window A window that contains the running PowerPoint application. The PowerPoint window includes the PowerPoint menus, toolbars, and Presentation window.

Presentation software A software program used to organize and present information.

Presentation window The area or "canvas" where you work and view your presentation. You type text and work with objects in the Presentation window.

Scale To change the size of a graphic a specific percentage of its original size.

Scroll To move within a window to see parts of a document that are not currently visible.

Selection box A slanted line border that appears around a text object or placeholder indicating it is ready to accept text.

Sizing handles The small squares at each corner of a selected object. Dragging a handle resizes the object.

Slide icon A symbol that appears next to a slide in Outline view.

Slide indicator box A small box that appears when you drag the vertical scroll box in Slide and Notes Page view identifying which slide you are on.

Slide Master A template for all slides in a presentation. Text and design elements you place on the slide master appear on every slide of the presentation. The title slide has its own master, called the Title Master (see also *Title Master*). There is also the Notes Master for Notes Page view and Handout Master for Slide Sorter view.

Slide miniature A reduced version of the current slide that appears in a small window.

Slide pane The presentation window section that contains a single slide, including text and graphics.

Slide Show view A view that shows a presentation as an electronic slide show.

Slide Sorter view A presentation view that provides a miniature picture of all slides in the order in which they appear in your presentation; used to rearrange slides and add special effects.

Slide view A presentation view with a large Slide pane and a reduced Outline pane.

Stacking order The order in which objects are placed on the slide. The first object placed on the slide is on the bottom, the last object placed on the slide is on the top.

Standard toolbar The toolbar containing the buttons that perform some of the most frequently used commands.

Status bar The bar at the bottom of the PowerPoint window that contains messages about what you are doing and seeing in PowerPoint, such as the current slide number or a description of a command or button.

Text anchor The location in a text object that determines the location of the text within the placeholder.

Text label A text object you create using the Text Box button.

Text object Any text you create using the Text Box button or enter into a placeholder. Once you enter text into a placeholder, the placeholder becomes a text object.

Text placeholder A box with a dashed border and text that you replace with your own text.

Timing The time a slide stays on the screen during a slide show.

Title The first line or heading on a slide.

Title Master A template for all title slides in a presentation. Text and design elements you place on the Title Master appear on all slides in the presentation that use the title slide layout.

Title placeholder A box on a slide reserved for the title of a presentation or slide.

Title slide The first slide in your presentation.

Toggle button A button that turns a feature on and off.

Transition The effect that moves one slide off the screen and the next slide on the screen during a slide show. Each slide can have its own transition effect.

View A way of looking at your presentation, such as Slide view, Normal view, Notes Page view, Slide Sorter view, and Slide Show view.

View buttons The buttons next to the horizontal scroll bar that you click to switch among views.

Window A rectangular area of the screen where you view and work on presentations.

Wizard An interactive set of dialog boxes that guides you through the process of creating a presentation; it asks you questions about presentation preferences and creates the presentation according to your specifications.

.wmf The abbreviation for the Windows metafile file format, which is the format of much clip art.

Word-processing box A text object you draw using the Text Box button that automatically wraps text inside a box.

Index

▶ A

adjustment handles
  for Arc drawing tool, POWERPOINT E-10–11

advanced drawing tools, POWERPOINT E-10–11

advanced formatting tools, POWERPOINT E-12–13

Align bottom button, POWERPOINT D-15

alignment
  of clip art, POWERPOINT D-2–3
  defined, POWERPOINT C-8
  of drawing objects with text, POWERPOINT C-6
  with guides, POWERPOINT C-10
  of objects, POWERPOINT C-8–9,
    POWERPOINT C-10–11

Align top button, POWERPOINT D-15

animation effects
  for slides, POWERPOINT D-18–19

animations
  graphics, POWERPOINT D-3

annotations
  on slides, POWERPOINT D-12–13

Apply Design Template dialog box,
  POWERPOINT B-5, POWERPOINT B-17,
  POWERPOINT E-5

Arc drawing tool, POWERPOINT E-10–11

area charts, POWERPOINT D-7

Arrange All command, POWERPOINT E-13

attributes
  replacing, POWERPOINT C-15

audience
  handouts for, POWERPOINT A-3,
    POWERPOINT A-16–17
  for presentations, POWERPOINT B-2

AutoContent Wizard, POWERPOINT A-6–7
  defined, POWERPOINT A-7
  Help information about, POWERPOINT A-14–15

AutoCorrect, POWERPOINT B-15,
  POWERPOINT C-18–19
  options, POWERPOINT C-19

AutoCorrect dialog box, POWERPOINT C-18–19

AutoLayouts
  Blank, POWERPOINT B-17
  Chart, POWERPOINT D-6
  creating new slides with, POWERPOINT B-8–9
  defined, POWERPOINT B-4
  placeholders in, POWERPOINT B-8–9
  selecting, POWERPOINT B-4
  Text & Clip Art, POWERPOINT D-2

AutoShape, POWERPOINT C-4
  text in, POWERPOINT C-6, POWERPOINT C-14

AutoShapes menu
  advanced drawing tools, POWERPOINT E-10–11

▶ B

backgrounds
  of pictures, POWERPOINT D-4
  predesigned, POWERPOINT C-16
  for presentations, POWERPOINT C-16–17

bar charts, POWERPOINT D-7

black-and-white presentations
  overheads, POWERPOINT A-3
  printing, POWERPOINT A-16–17
  viewing, POWERPOINT A-17

black slides, POWERPOINT D-16

Blank AutoLayout, POWERPOINT B-17

Blank presentation dialog box, POWERPOINT A-7

Border Color button, POWERPOINT D-15

Borders button, POWERPOINT D-15

Border Style button, POWERPOINT D-15

Border Width button, POWERPOINT D-15

bubble charts, POWERPOINT D-7

Bulleted List placeholder, POWERPOINT B-9

bullets
  formatting in master view, POWERPOINT E-4–5

Bullets and Numbering dialog box,
  POWERPOINT E-4–5

buttons
  removing from toolbars, POWERPOINT E-16

▶ C

cells
  in Graph datasheets, POWERPOINT D-6–7

Center button, POWERPOINT D-14,
  POWERPOINT D-15

Center Vertically button, POWERPOINT D-14,
  POWERPOINT D-15

Change/Change All option
  in spell checker, POWERPOINT B-15

Chart AutoLayout, POWERPOINT D-6

Chart Formatting toolbar, POWERPOINT D-10

Chart placeholder, POWERPOINT B-9,
  POWERPOINT D-6

charts, POWERPOINT D-1
  customizing, POWERPOINT D-10
  embedding, POWERPOINT D-6–7
  types of, POWERPOINT D-7

circles
  drawing, POWERPOINT C-4

clip art, POWERPOINT D-1. *See also* graphics;
  pictures
  aligning, POWERPOINT D-2–3
  gallery, POWERPOINT D-2–3
  inserting in slides, POWERPOINT D-2–3
  sources of, POWERPOINT D-2
  Web sources, POWERPOINT D-2–3

Clip Art placeholder, POWERPOINT B-9

Clip Gallery. *See* Microsoft Clip Gallery

closing presentations, POWERPOINT A-16–17

Collapse All button, POWERPOINT B-11

Collapse button, POWERPOINT B-11

color
  in drawing objects, POWERPOINT C-4
  of fonts, POWERPOINT C-14
  overheads, POWERPOINT A-3
  in presentations, POWERPOINT B-16–17

Color Scheme dialog box, POWERPOINT C-16–17

Index

color schemes
  applying to another presentation, POWERPOINT E-13
  applying to selected slides, POWERPOINT C-16
  elements, POWERPOINT C-17
  for presentations, POWERPOINT C-16—17

column charts, POWERPOINT D-7

columns, in datasheets
  resizing, POWERPOINT D-8
  Series in Columns, POWERPOINT D-9

Common Tasks menu, POWERPOINT A-8, POWERPOINT D-2

cone charts, POWERPOINT D-7

Connector line tool, POWERPOINT E-10

context-sensitive Help, POWERPOINT A-15

copying
  drawing objects, POWERPOINT C-6—7
  with Office Clipboard, POWERPOINT C-7

criteria
  specifying for file searches, POWERPOINT C-3

Crop button, POWERPOINT D-4

cropping pictures, POWERPOINT D-4—5

cropping tool, POWERPOINT D-4

Currency Style button, POWERPOINT D-10

Curve drawing tool, POWERPOINT E-10

Custom Animation dialog box, POWERPOINT D-18—19

Customize command
  customizing toolbars with, POWERPOINT E-16—17

Customize dialog box, POWERPOINT E-16—17

customized toolbars
  creating, POWERPOINT E-16—17

cylinder charts, POWERPOINT D-7

▶ D

data label columns
  sizing, POWERPOINT D-8

data labels, POWERPOINT D-6—7, POWERPOINT D-8—9

data markers, POWERPOINT D-8

data series, POWERPOINT D-6—7
  formatting, POWERPOINT D-10

data series markers, POWERPOINT D-6—7

datasheets
  defined, POWERPOINT D-6—7
  entering data in, POWERPOINT D-8—9

datasheet window, POWERPOINT D-6, POWERPOINT D-8

Decrease Decimal button, POWERPOINT D-10

defaults
  filename placeholder, POWERPOINT A-12
  toolbars, POWERPOINT A-9

deleting slides, POWERPOINT B-8

Demote button, POWERPOINT B-10, POWERPOINT B-11

design
  evaluating, POWERPOINT B-16—17
  of presentations, POWERPOINT B-2—3, POWERPOINT B-16—17

design templates
  applying to existing presentations, POWERPOINT B-5
  creating, POWERPOINT B-17
  defined, POWERPOINT A-7, POWERPOINT B-1, POWERPOINT B-4
  modifying, POWERPOINT B-17
  selecting, POWERPOINT B-4—5

Dissolve, POWERPOINT D-18

doughnut charts, POWERPOINT D-7

Draw menu, POWERPOINT C-8—9, POWERPOINT C-10

Draw menu button, POWERPOINT C-5

Draw Table button, POWERPOINT D-15

drawing objects
  aligning with text, POWERPOINT C-6
  copying, POWERPOINT C-6—7
  creating, POWERPOINT C-4—5
  editing, POWERPOINT C-6—7

Drawing toolbar, POWERPOINT A-8—9, POWERPOINT C-4—5
  buttons, POWERPOINT C-5

drawing tools, POWERPOINT E-10—11

▶ E

embedding
  charts, POWERPOINT D-6—7
  defined, POWERPOINT D-6

Embed TrueType fonts option, POWERPOINT A-12

Eraser button, POWERPOINT D-15

Excel. *See* Microsoft Excel

exceptions
  to Slide Masters, POWERPOINT E-7

exiting
  PowerPoint 2000, POWERPOINT A-16—17

Expand All button, POWERPOINT B-11

▶ F

Fade Through Black option, POWERPOINT D-16

filenames
  default filename placeholder, POWERPOINT A-12

files
  searching for, by properties, POWERPOINT C-3

Fill color button, POWERPOINT D-15

Fill Color drawing tool, POWERPOINT D-5

Fill Color list arrow, POWERPOINT C-4, POWERPOINT D-14

Fill Effects dialog box, POWERPOINT C-16—17, POWERPOINT E-12

flipping objects, POWERPOINT C-11

Font Color list arrow, POWERPOINT C-14

Font list, POWERPOINT C-14, POWERPOINT C-15

font size, POWERPOINT B-16—17, POWERPOINT C-14

fonts
  applying to master text, POWERPOINT E-4—5
  color, POWERPOINT C-14
  in presentations, POWERPOINT B-16—17
  saving with presentation, POWERPOINT A-12
  selecting, POWERPOINT C-14

footers
  in slides, POWERPOINT B-13
  spell checking, POWERPOINT B-14

Format AutoShape dialog box, POWERPOINT E-8—9

Format Data Series dialog box, POWERPOINT D-10,

Format Painter, POWERPOINT E-12—13

Format Painter button, POWERPOINT E-12

Format Picture button, POWERPOINT D-4

Format Table dialog box, POWERPOINT D-14

formatting
  advanced tools, POWERPOINT E-12—13
  charts, POWERPOINT D-10—11
  master text, POWERPOINT E-4—5
  tables, POWERPOINT D-14

text in master view, POWERPOINT E-4—5

text in slides, POWERPOINT C-14—15

Formatting toolbar, POWERPOINT A-8

More Buttons button, POWERPOINT A-9

restoring defaults, POWERPOINT A-9

freeform shapes

drawing, POWERPOINT E-11

►G

gallery, POWERPOINT D-2—3

Graph Gradient tab, Fill Effects dialog box, POWERPOINT C-16—17

chart types, POWERPOINT D-7

creating charts with, POWERPOINT D-6—7

formatting charts, POWERPOINT D-10—11

graphics. *See also* clip art; pictures

file formats, POWERPOINT D-5

saving slides as, POWERPOINT D-5

graph objects

embedding in slides, POWERPOINT D-6—7

Grayscale checkbox, POWERPOINT A-16

Grayscale Preview button, POWERPOINT A-17

Group command, POWERPOINT C-10, POWERPOINT D-5

grouping objects, POWERPOINT C-8—9, POWERPOINT C-10—11

guides

aligning objects with, POWERPOINT C-10

►H

Handout Master view, POWERPOINT E-2

handouts, POWERPOINT A-3

printing, POWERPOINT A-16—17

hanging indents, POWERPOINT E-6

headers

in slides, POWERPOINT B-13

height

of pictures, POWERPOINT D-4

Height up arrow, POWERPOINT D-4

Help

context sensitive, POWERPOINT A-15

PowerPoint 2000, POWERPOINT A-14—15

horizontal ruler

changing text indents with, POWERPOINT E-6—7

►I

Ignore/Ignore All option

in spell checker, POWERPOINT B-15

Increase Font Size button, POWERPOINT C-14

indent markers, POWERPOINT E-6—7

indents

changing levels in master view, POWERPOINT E-6—7

hanging, POWERPOINT E-6

Insert Clip Art button, POWERPOINT D-2

Insert ClipArt dialog box, POWERPOINT D-3

Insert Clip icon, POWERPOINT D-2

insertion point

in placeholders, POWERPOINT B-6

Insert Menu and Table slide layout, POWERPOINT D-14

Insert Object dialog box, POWERPOINT D-4—5

italic text, POWERPOINT C-14

►K

keyboard controls

for slide shows, POWERPOINT D-13

►L

leading, POWERPOINT E-8—9

light bulbs

in PowerPoint Help system, POWERPOINT A-15

line charts, POWERPOINT D-7

Line Color list arrow, POWERPOINT C-4

lines

drawing with annotation pen, POWERPOINT D-12—13

line spacing

adjusting, POWERPOINT E-8—9

Line Spacing dialog box, POWERPOINT E-8—9

Lock aspect ratio, POWERPOINT D-4

►M

main text placeholder, POWERPOINT B-6—7

margins

adjusting, POWERPOINT E-8—9

Master Layout dialog box, POWERPOINT E-3

master placeholders, POWERPOINT E-2—3

reapplying, POWERPOINT E-3

master text

formatting, POWERPOINT E-4—5

Master text placeholder, POWERPOINT E-2—3

Master title placeholder, POWERPOINT E-2—3

Media Clip placeholder, POWERPOINT B-9

menu bar, POWERPOINT A-8—9

Merge Cells button, POWERPOINT D-15

Microsoft Clip Gallery, POWERPOINT D-2—3

Microsoft Clip Gallery dialog box, POWERPOINT D-2—3

Microsoft Clip Gallery Live Web site, POWERPOINT D-3

Microsoft Graph. *See* Graph

Microsoft Word

importing text into presentations from, POWERPOINT C-13

More Buttons button, POWERPOINT A-9

mouse pointer shapes, POWERPOINT B-7, POWERPOINT D-12

Move Down button, POWERPOINT B-11

Move Up button, POWERPOINT B-10, POWERPOINT B-11

►N

New Presentation dialog box, POWERPOINT B-4—5

tabs, POWERPOINT B-4

New Slide dialog box, POWERPOINT B-8—9

New Toolbar dialog box, POWERPOINT E-16—17

Normal view, POWERPOINT A-8

viewing presentations in, POWERPOINT A-10—11

working in, POWERPOINT B-4

Normal View button, POWERPOINT B-12

notes

entering, POWERPOINT B-12—13

Notes Master view, POWERPOINT E-2

Notes Page view, POWERPOINT A-10, POWERPOINT B-12—13

viewing presentations in, POWERPOINT A-10—11

Notes pane, POWERPOINT A-8, POWERPOINT B-12—13

viewing, POWERPOINT A-10

Index

►O

Object placeholder, POWERPOINT B-9

objects. *See also* text objects

aligning, POWERPOINT C-8—9, POWERPOINT C-10—11

clip art, POWERPOINT D-2—3

defined, POWERPOINT B-6

drawing, POWERPOINT C-4—5, POWERPOINT C-6—7

editing, POWERPOINT C-6—7

flipping, POWERPOINT C-11

graph, POWERPOINT D-6—7

grouping, POWERPOINT C-8—9, POWERPOINT C-10—11

modifying, POWERPOINT C-4—5

placeholders as, POWERPOINT B-6

resizing, POWERPOINT C-4—5

rotating, POWERPOINT C-11

stacking, POWERPOINT C-8—9

three-dimensional, POWERPOINT C-11

Office Assistant, POWERPOINT A-8

light bulbs in, POWERPOINT A-15

Style Checker and, POWERPOINT E-14—15

Office Clipboard

copying objects with, POWERPOINT C-7

online meetings, POWERPOINT A-3

On mouse click check box, POWERPOINT D-16

on-screen presentations, POWERPOINT A-3

Open an existing presentation dialog box, POWERPOINT A-7

Open dialog box, POWERPOINT C-2—3

Organization Chart placeholder, POWERPOINT B-9

outline pages, POWERPOINT A-3

Outline pane, POWERPOINT A-8

text display in, POWERPOINT B-6

viewing, POWERPOINT A-10

Outline view

viewing presentations in, POWERPOINT A-10—11

working in, POWERPOINT B-10—11

Outline View button, POWERPOINT A-10, POWERPOINT B-10

Outlining toolbar

buttons, POWERPOINT B-11

using in Outline view, POWERPOINT B-10—11

Oval button, POWERPOINT C-4

►P

panes

in PowerPoint windows, POWERPOINT A-8—9

paragraphs

adjusting spacing around, POWERPOINT E-8—9

Pen tool, POWERPOINT D-12

pictures, POWERPOINT D-1. *See also* clip art; graphics

cropping, POWERPOINT D-4—5

inserting, POWERPOINT D-4—5

recoloring, POWERPOINT D-5

scaling, POWERPOINT D-4—5

ungrouping, POWERPOINT D-5

pie charts, POWERPOINT D-7

placeholders

in AutoLayouts, POWERPOINT B-8—9

chart, POWERPOINT D-6

in Slide Masters, POWERPOINT E-2—3

text, POWERPOINT B-6—7

.pot file extension, POWERPOINT B-17

PowerPoint 2000

creating a shortcut for, POWERPOINT A-4

exiting, POWERPOINT A-16—17

features, POWERPOINT A-2—3

Help, POWERPOINT A-14—15

installation type, POWERPOINT A-6

starting, POWERPOINT A-4—5

uses of, POWERPOINT A-1, POWERPOINT A-2—3

PowerPoint startup dialog box, POWERPOINT A-4—5, POWERPOINT A-6

PowerPoint Viewer, POWERPOINT A-2

PowerPoint window. *See also* presentation windows

panes, POWERPOINT A-8—9

viewing, POWERPOINT A-8—9

Presentation options screen, POWERPOINT A-6

presentations. *See also* slides

backgrounds, POWERPOINT C-16—17

checking spelling in, POWERPOINT B-14—15

checklist, POWERPOINT D-19

closing, POWERPOINT A-16—17

color schemes, POWERPOINT C-16—17

creating, POWERPOINT B-1—17

creating with AutoContent Wizard, POWERPOINT A-6—7

customizing, POWERPOINT E-1—17

design of, POWERPOINT B-16—17

design templates for, POWERPOINT B-1, POWERPOINT B-4—5

determining output type, POWERPOINT B-2

enhancing, POWERPOINT D-1—19

evaluating, POWERPOINT B-16—17

modifying, POWERPOINT C-1—19

naming different versions of, POWERPOINT C-2

opening, POWERPOINT C-2—3

planning, POWERPOINT B-2—3

preparing for, POWERPOINT D-19

printing, POWERPOINT A-16—7

printing in black and white, POWERPOINT A-16—17

revising, POWERPOINT C-2—3

saving, POWERPOINT A-12—13

saving copies of, POWERPOINT C-2—3

saving fonts with, POWERPOINT A-12

showing, POWERPOINT D-12—13

tables for, POWERPOINT D-14—15

types of, POWERPOINT A-3

viewing, POWERPOINT A-10—11, POWERPOINT B-16

viewing in black and white, POWERPOINT A-17

viewing in gray scale, POWERPOINT A-16, POWERPOINT A-17

visual elements of, POWERPOINT B-16—17

presentation software, POWERPOINT A-2—3

Presentation style screen, POWERPOINT A-6

Presentation type screen, POWERPOINT A-6

Presentation windows, POWERPOINT A-8. *See also* PowerPoint window

arranging side-by-side, POWERPOINT E-13

Preset option

selecting predesigned backgrounds with, POWERPOINT C-16

Previous Slide button, POWERPOINT A-10, POWERPOINT B-10

Print dialog box, POWERPOINT A-16—17

printing

black-and-white presentations, POWERPOINT A-16—17

handouts, POWERPOINT A-16—17

presentations, POWERPOINT A-16—17

slides as transparencies, POWERPOINT A-16

Programs menu, POWERPOINT A-4—5

Promote button, POWERPOINT B-11

properties

defined, POWERPOINT C-3

searching for presentation files by, POWERPOINT C-3

Pure black and white check box, POWERPOINT A-16—17

pyramid charts, POWERPOINT D-7

▶ R

radar charts, POWERPOINT D-7

recoloring graphics, POWERPOINT D-5

Rectangle button, POWERPOINT C-4

red, wavy lines

indicating spelling errors, POWERPOINT B-12, POWERPOINT B-15

Rehearsal dialog box, POWERPOINT D-17

rehearsal slide show timing, POWERPOINT D-17

replacing text and attributes, POWERPOINT C-15

resizing objects, POWERPOINT C-4—5

rotating objects, POWERPOINT C-11

rows, in datasheets

Series in Rows, POWERPOINT D-9

rulers

aligning objects with, POWERPOINT C-6

▶ S

Save As dialog box, POWERPOINT A-12—13, POWERPOINT C-2—3, POWERPOINT D-5

Save button, POWERPOINT A-12

saving under another name, POWERPOINT A-12—13, POWERPOINT C-2—3, POWERPOINT D-5

presentations, POWERPOINT A-12—13

slides as graphics, POWERPOINT D-5

scaling pictures, POWERPOINT D-4—5

scatter (xy) charts, POWERPOINT D-7

selection box

around placeholders, POWERPOINT B-6

Series in Columns, POWERPOINT D-9

Series in Rows, POWERPOINT D-9

Set Transparent Color button, POWERPOINT D-4

shading

in slides, POWERPOINT C-16

shapes

freeform, drawing, POWERPOINT E-11

for text, changing margins around, POWERPOINT E-9

shortcuts

creating for PowerPoint, POWERPOINT A-4

Show Formatting button, POWERPOINT B-11

sizing handles

of Arc drawing tool, POWERPOINT E-10—11

resizing objects with, POWERPOINT C-4—5

Slide Finder dialog box, POWERPOINT C-12

slide icons, POWERPOINT A-10, POWERPOINT B-10

moving, POWERPOINT B-10

Slide Layout dialog box, POWERPOINT D-2

Slide Masters

applying from other presentations, POWERPOINT E-5

changing master text indents, POWERPOINT E-6—7

exceptions to, POWERPOINT E-7

features, POWERPOINT E-2—3

formatting text, POWERPOINT E-4—5

removing master graphics, POWERPOINT E-7

Slide Master view, POWERPOINT E-2

Master Layout dialog box, POWERPOINT E-3

Slide Navigator dialog box, POWERPOINT D-12

Slide options button, POWERPOINT A-16

Slide pane, POWERPOINT A-8

entering text in, POWERPOINT B-6

viewing, POWERPOINT A-10

slides, POWERPOINT A-2—3. *See also* presentations

animation effects, POWERPOINT D-18—19

annotations on, POWERPOINT D-12—13

backgrounds, POWERPOINT C-16—17

black, POWERPOINT D-16

checking spelling in, POWERPOINT B-14—15

clip art in, POWERPOINT D-2—3

color schemes, POWERPOINT C-16—17

creating, POWERPOINT B-8—9

deleting, POWERPOINT B-8

entering text into, POWERPOINT B-6—7

formatting text in, POWERPOINT C-14—15

headers and footers in, POWERPOINT B-13

inserting from other presentations, POWERPOINT C-12

printing as transparencies, POWERPOINT A-16

saving as graphics, POWERPOINT D-5

35-mm, POWERPOINT A-3

slides (35-mm), POWERPOINT A-3

exporting slides to, POWERPOINT H-3

Slide Show button, POWERPOINT A-10, POWERPOINT B-16, POWERPOINT D-16

slide shows

keyboard controls, POWERPOINT D-13

timings, POWERPOINT D-16—17

transitions, POWERPOINT D-16—17

viewing, POWERPOINT D-12—13

Slide Show view, POWERPOINT D-12—13

viewing presentations in, POWERPOINT A-10—11

Slide Sorter view, POWERPOINT D-16—17, POWERPOINT D-18—19

viewing presentations in, POWERPOINT A-10—11

Slide Sorter View button, POWERPOINT A-10, POWERPOINT B-16

slide timings, POWERPOINT D-16—17

rehearsal, POWERPOINT D-17

Slide Transition dialog box, POWERPOINT D-16—17

slide transitions, POWERPOINT D-16—17

Slide view

viewing presentations in, POWERPOINT A-10—11

working in, POWERPOINT B-4

Slide View button, POWERPOINT A-10

sound clips, POWERPOINT D-2, POWERPOINT D-3

speaker notes, POWERPOINT A-3

spell checking

presentations, POWERPOINT B-14—15

as you write, POWERPOINT B-12, POWERPOINT B-15

Spelling dialog box, POWERPOINT B-14—15

spelling errors

indicated by red, wavy lines, POWERPOINT B-12, POWERPOINT B-15

Split Cells button, POWERPOINT D-15

squares

drawing, POWERPOINT C-4

stacking objects, POWERPOINT C-8—9

Standard toolbar, POWERPOINT A-8—9

More Buttons button, POWERPOINT A-9

restoring defaults, POWERPOINT A-9

Stars and Banners, POWERPOINT C-4

Start button, POWERPOINT A-4

status bar, POWERPOINT A-8—9

Index

stock charts, POWERPOINT D-7

Style Checker, POWERPOINT E-14—15

Style Options dialog box, POWERPOINT E-14—15

Suggest option
    in spell checker, POWERPOINT B-15

Summary Slide button, POWERPOINT B-11

surface charts, POWERPOINT D-7

►T

Table menu button, POWERPOINT D-15

Table placeholder, POWERPOINT B-9

tables
    creating, POWERPOINT D-14—15
    formatting, POWERPOINT D-14

Tables and Borders toolbar, POWERPOINT D-14—15
    buttons on, POWERPOINT D-15

templates. *See* design templates; Slide Masters

text. *See also* text objects
    advanced editing capabilities,
        POWERPOINT C-12—13
    aligning drawing objects with,
        POWERPOINT C-6
    correcting automatically, POWERPOINT C-18—19
    entered in AutoShapes, POWERPOINT C-6
    entering in slides, POWERPOINT B-6—7
    formatting, POWERPOINT C-14—15
    formatting in master view, POWERPOINT E-4—5
    importing from Word, POWERPOINT C-13
    replacing, POWERPOINT C-15
    in shapes, changing margins around,
        POWERPOINT E-9
    wrapping in an AutoShape, POWERPOINT C-14

text anchors, POWERPOINT E-8—9

Text Box button, POWERPOINT C-12

Text & Clip Art AutoLayout, POWERPOINT D-2

text objects. *See also* objects; text

adjusting, POWERPOINT E-8—9
    placeholders as, POWERPOINT B-6
    selecting, POWERPOINT C-12

text placeholders, POWERPOINT B-6—7

35-mm slides, POWERPOINT A-3

3-D button, POWERPOINT C-11

three-dimensional (3-D) objects, POWERPOINT C-11

timings. *See* slide timings

title bar, POWERPOINT A-8—9

Title Master view, POWERPOINT E-2
    Master Layout dialog box, POWERPOINT E-3

title placeholder, POWERPOINT B-6—7

titles
    in Outline View, POWERPOINT B-10
    text color, POWERPOINT C-17

title slides, POWERPOINT B-4
    entering text in, POWERPOINT B-6—7

toolbars, POWERPOINT A-8—9
    creating, POWERPOINT E-16—17
    customizing, POWERPOINT E-16—17
    removing buttons from, POWERPOINT E-16
    restoring defaults, POWERPOINT A-9

transition icon, POWERPOINT D-16

transitions
    for slide shows, POWERPOINT D-16—17

transparencies, POWERPOINT A-3
    printing slides as, POWERPOINT A-16

TrueType fonts
    embedding, POWERPOINT A-12

►U

ungrouping pictures, POWERPOINT D-5

Update Link command, POWERPOINT E-16

Up Ribbon button, POWERPOINT C-4

►V

vertical guides
    aligning objects with, POWERPOINT C-10

view buttons, POWERPOINT A-8—9

views, POWERPOINT A-8—9

voice narrations

►W

wavy, red lines
    indicating spelling errors, POWERPOINT B-12,
        POWERPOINT B-15

Web presentations, POWERPOINT A-3

Width
    of pictures, POWERPOINT D-4

Windows metafile format, POWERPOINT D-5

wizards
    AutoContent Wizard, POWERPOINT A-6—7,
        POWERPOINT A-14—15
    defined, POWERPOINT A-6
    PowerPoint installation type and,
        POWERPOINT A-6

.wmf filename extension, POWERPOINT D-5

Word. *See* Microsoft Word

►X

X-axis, POWERPOINT D-10—11

XY (scatter) charts, POWERPOINT D-7

►Z

Z-axis, POWERPOINT D-10—11

Zoom list arrow, POWERPOINT B-12

Zoom text box, POWERPOINT D-18